I0413471

Smoking

ALSO BY ERIC COATES

Hearing Voices: A Memoir of Madness

*Cracking Up: A Memoir of Love, Drinking, Drugs,
Poverty, Paranoia and Other Afflictions of a Life
on the Road to Madness*

*Memos: Advice to a Young Executive on the Art of Lying,
Twisting the Facts, and Using the Media
for Your Own Selfish Purposes*

Smoking

An Intimate History

Eric Coates

SMOKING Copyright © 2014 by Eric Coates.
No part of this publication may be reproduced,
stored in a retrieval system or transmitted in any form
or by any means without the prior written permission
of the publisher.

Cover image "Smoke" Copyright 2009 by Brenton Doyle.

A custome lothsome to the eye, hatefull to the Nose, harmefull to the braine, dangerous to the Lungs, and in the blacke stinking fume thereof, neerest resembling the horrible Stigian smoke of the pit that is bottomelesse.

— King James VI of Scotland and I of England, from *A Counterblaste to Tobacco*

If one were to search for similarities among the fifty-six men who drew up the birth certificate of the most powerful nation in history, one would discover a belief in God, and tobacco interests.

— Iain Gately on the signers of the Declaration of Independence, from *Tobacco: A Cultural History of How an Exotic Plant Seduced Civilization*

Introduction

I am neither a historian nor a scholar. This is not intended to be a comprehensive history of tobacco and smoking. Nevertheless it seems important to make mention, at least roughly, of how smoking spread around the globe. I have put together an informal list of how tobacco reached different countries, derived from my reading on the subject. One thing is clear: at a time when people depended on horses and sailing ships, when anything you wanted to carry you had to actually carry, tobacco spread around the world with amazing rapidity.

The villains of this story of the spread of smoking around the globe are most often the Portuguese, the Spanish and the Dutch. All three did their best to introduce tobacco to the countries they visited and traded with. Besides going to the Americas, where tobacco had been chewed and smoked and sniffed for thousands of years, Portuguese merchants traveled the coast of Africa (where tobacco spread with a speed that would take your breath away), went along the edge of the Indian Ocean, and visited the nations of East Asia, most notably China. For this reason tobacco reached Japan at roughly the same time as it reached most of Europe, thousands of miles to the west of Japan and that much closer to where tobacco originated in the Americas. The Spanish brought tobacco to the Philippines, whence it spread to Cambodia, Thailand, Sri Lanka and eventually India. The Dutch spread it wherever they could — basically, wherever the Portuguese and Spanish hadn't. Once introduced, tobacco spread from countries that had it to countries that didn't. It was that simple. It was enough to introduce the weed to be sure that people would want more of it and thus to assure that trade would continue.

It is thought that at the beginning of this time the real smokers were sailors on ships, who passed on the habit of smoking to each other. Sailors from the time of Columbus's voyage to the Americas in 1492 picked up the habit from Native Americans and ever after took it with them wherever they went. Later, Portuguese trading posts began raising crops of tobacco, which are believed to have been given to sailors at first but which eventually grew into plantations that produced tobacco that could be sold.

Each of the countries that received tobacco rapidly integrated it into their culture. Many cultures, particularly in Africa, developed myths around it as though it had been with them since times immemorial. One example of this phenomenon is the legend of Van Hunks and Table Mountain. There are several versions of this myth, but the basic elements are always the same. The legend goes that Jan Van Hunks, a Dutch pirate who lived in the early years of the 18th century, retired from his life at sea and went to live at a place called Devil's Peak, near Table Mountain. Every day he would climb the mountain — to get away from a nagging wife, it is said — and would settle down at his favorite place to smoke his pipe. One day, as he came to his usual place, he was surprised to discover a man already sitting at the exact place where he always sat. The man was dressed in black and he wore a large-brimmed hat, pulled down to hide most of his face. Van Hunks sat down next to the man and the two of them began to talk. Van Hunks liked to brag, and he smoked an un-usually strong tobacco, and as he lit up his pipe he started to brag that no one else could smoke as much of his tobacco as he did. The other man said that he could easily smoke as much as Van Hunks. Van Hunks felt a little annoyed at this, and he immediately chal-lenged the man to a kind of duel: which one of them could smoke the most of his tobacco? He put a huge pile of his tobacco between them and the two of them filled their pipes and began to smoke. They smoked so much that soon they were surrounded by a huge cloud of smoke. The cloud was so big, in fact, that it began to creep up over the mountain and spread across it. Soon the whole top of the mountain was covered with a cloud of smoke. People who lived in the town below looked up and saw the cloud of smoke and were amazed. Van Hunks and the stranger kept smoking and smoking — some people say for several days. When finally the stranger couldn't take any more and he fell to the ground in a stupor, his hat fell off and revealed a set of horns. Van Hunks had been smoking with the devil. Angry to have been beaten by a mere human, the devil clapped his hands and in an instant, with a loud clap of thunder, both of them vanished in a puff of smoke, leaving behind only a scorched patch of ground. Legend has it that the cloud of tobacco smoke they left behind became what is known as the "Table Cloth" — the famous white cloud that spills over Table Mountain when the southeaster blows in summer. When that happens, it is said that Van Hunks and the Devil are at it again.

Starting from the Americas in 1492, tobacco had established itself around the globe by about 1650.

*

As I said, I am neither a historian nor a scholar. I'm not even an expert on smoking. What I am is a smoker, which I suppose is its own kind of expertise. One day, after more than thirty years of smoking, I took a look at the butt I was smoking and thought, basically, *What the hell is this thing really? I don't know a thing about it.* The fact is that I was just curious. After decades of daily exposure to cigarettes, I didn't know anything about their history, I didn't know who invented them or where they came from or even what was in them really. And that's a pretty strange thing for something you've been as intimately involved with as I have been with cigarettes all these years. I spend hours every day smoking. I've given years of my life to the practice. It's the first thing I do in the morning and the last thing I do at night. And yet I had not a clue about it.

I didn't really set out to write this book. I just went on the Internet and looked up some books about smoking and then I went down to the library and ordered them. If you're going to find out about smoking, I figured, you might as well learn something about tobacco, so that's where I started. I didn't plan on doing a bunch of research, like I said, but as I started reading — *Hey, this stuff's pretty interesting!* — I just kept looking up and ordering more books. And with little more than an Internet connection and a library card, I started to explore a topic that has gotten more and more fascinating as I've gone along. After a while I started taking notes. After all, I'm not unique; and if I found it all pretty interesting, I figured there would be someone else out there who would find it pretty interesting too.

While I was at it, I realized that I was missing a big part of the story: that is, what it's like to actually be a smoker? So I started making some notes on that too. After all, I've been smoking more than thirty years. Why shouldn't I share some of what I've learned about *that*? And why not just put down some information that applies to any smoker anywhere? Smoking itself is pretty fascinating. All of that information ended up in the even-numbered chapters, in between all the chapters about tobacco and cigarettes. If you're a smoker, you can probably relate. If you're not, well, here's a little bit of what it's like, in case you were wondering.

Think of this book, then, as a very personal report on tobacco and smoking — sort of a memoir and a history put together. You could have found all this information yourself, but hey, you don't have to: I've put it together for you. If you really want to know about smoking and cigarettes, it's probably a good idea to start off with some information about the history of tobacco, so that's where I started out. It all leads pretty quickly to smoking. And I promise you: it gets more interesting as you go along. Once it really started to become a story, I could hardly wait to get my hands on the next book, the next source of information. And you may be surprised to see what it says about smoking in the end — about us, really. It certainly opened my eyes.

And with that we can get to the book. I hope you find it all as compelling as I did.

1.

Tobacco has a long history in the Americas. It is here that it was first discovered, used and cultivated by Native Americans. It was America's first commercial crop back when America still consisted of a few scattered colonies. Although Spaniards grew tobacco for trade and profit before the English — indeed had cornered much of the world market in tobacco — the first capitalist of the British colonies to cash in on tobacco was John Rolfe, who survived a hurricane at sea, shipwreck on the reefs of the Bahamas, and the deaths of his wife and daughter, and then in spite of all this became a successful planter of tobacco in the Jamestown colony. (Later he became the husband of Pocahontas.) Rolfe planted tobacco with seeds he had somehow acquired from the Spaniards, probably from the planters of Trinidad. He carefully studied how to raise and cure tobacco, with the result that the Virginia colony, where not long before colonists had been starving or killed off by Native Americans, began to show a profit with its shipments of tobacco to England. Rolfe first planted tobacco in 1612. By 1618, the colony sent a tobacco crop of 20,000 pounds back to England. By 1622, only four years later, the colony had a crop of 60,000 pounds. By 1627, the colony sent 500,000 pounds back to England, and by 1629, just two years later, that amount tripled to 1,500,000 pounds.

It is not too much to say that tobacco saved the early colonists.

*

When I was growing up in the 1970s and 80s there was still a lot of tobacco grown in New England. When people think of tobacco, they most often think of southern states like Virginia; the light tobacco that most people smoke, even that grown in other states, is called "Virginia" in the trade. But tobacco has been grown in New England since ancient times. As the New York *Times* reported in an old article, "Tobacco-Growing in Connecticut,"

> There appears to be a stretch of peculiar soil and conditions of growth, with a suitable climate, extending from the Long Island Sound through the river valleys of Connecticut, over Massachusetts, even into the States of New-Hampshire and Vermont, remarkably favorable to the growth of a certain kind of tobacco. This tobacco is so much in demand that it is mainly used for the wrappers

of Havana and West India cigars — these latter being specially valued even in foreign countries, where they have coverings from this excellent New-England plant. What is remarkable about it is that there is no other tobacco in the country, not even that of Virginia and Kentucky, which can take the place of the Connecticut leaf.

The varieties of tobacco still grown in New England are the kinds known as broadleaf and shade, the varieties used for the best cigar wrappers and binders. It's grown chiefly in the Connecticut River Valley, which divides Vermont and New Hampshire and extends down through Massachusetts and Connecticut to the ocean, and has been grown there since long before the colonists arrived.

New England tobacco has not been a crop that was raised on the side or by amateurs. This was big business. In 1949, 26.3 million pounds of tobacco were harvested in Connecticut and 13.6 million pounds were harvested in Massachusetts. That's a total of 39.9 million pounds, which, needless to say, is a lot of tobacco.

It is still possible to drive along the highways of the Connecticut River Valley and see fields of tobacco and the sheds where it is dried, but this is growing less common as farmers switch to other crops or stop growing altogether. A friend of mine tells me that when he was young, in the 1950s and 60s, it was not uncommon for young people to work in the fields alongside migrant workers; there are still some migrant workers, mostly from Jamaica, who show up every year to help with the crop. But this is changing. As of 2013, the crop is down about ninety per cent from its peak in the 1940s.

Times change. There just aren't as many people smoking in the United States as there used to be, and the rest of the world, which used to rely on the United States for so much of its tobacco, is now getting the bulk of its supply from other countries. But if tobacco has declined in New England, indeed is losing ground all over the United States, it is still getting bigger — might even be said to be exploding — around most of the world.

2.

The first thing I remember about cigarettes is going to my father's house. My mother and he had separated and divorced when I was very young and I went to see him every other weekend. Every other weekend he and his new wife came to pick us up. They packed us into the back seat of a small car and proceeded to light up, again and again, for the hour and change that it took to get to their house. I remember sitting in the back seat, listening to their eight-track, sometimes barely able to breathe because of the smoke. I was maybe six years old at the time.

My stepfather and mother smoked intermittently. They were the sort of people who lit up a cigarette, took a couple puffs, put it in the ashtray and forgot about it. All the ashtrays were full of these barely-smoked butts. They smoked menthols or those absurdly thin cigarettes that are marketed to women or were marketed to women back then.

Doctors smoked back then. Nurses smoked back then. You could smoke on airplanes and trains and in taxis and elevators. In public buildings there were ashtrays attached to the walls.

*

I do not remember having a lot of thoughts about smoking. It was just something that was there like the sky and the kitchen furniture. It was just a fact.

I do not remember being particularly interested in smoking, in fact, until I started smoking.

Some weekends I went to see my father's parents and some weekends I went to see my mother's parents. Both sets of grandparents were just a few miles away. My mother's parents smoked. If memory serves, my grand-father smoked Camels and my step-grandmother (my real grandmother had died young) smoked Merits.

My grandfather died when I was seven. All I remember of him is his scratchy beard when he kissed us goodnight at bedtime and that he would threaten me with "the strap" — which never materialized — when I misbehaved.

After my grandfather died we didn't go to see my step-grandmother as much, but when we did we spent the whole weekend. And naturally enough, since she chain-smoked, there were packs of cigarettes lying around all over the place.

And being kids — who are naturally curious — eventually we decided to take some and try them out.

We did not realize you needed to inhale. We thought it was enough to suck the smoke into our mouths, wait a few seconds and then blow it out slowly as though we'd inhaled it. We had no clue. We were what? Eight? Nine years old? Naturally we had no idea what we were doing.

3.

The basic facts of tobacco are easy enough to enumerate. According to the website of the International Tobacco Growers' Association (ITGA):

> It is the world's most widely cultivated non-food crop and is chosen by farmers from more than 120 countries because of its performance under widely varying climatic (merely requiring a frost-free period of 100–130 days) and soil conditions.

Both of the plants that produce what we call tobacco belong to the genus *Nicotiana* — the species *tabacum*, which produces the lighter, smoother tobacco most people prefer, and the species *rustica*, which produces a heavier tobacco that is used less often. Richard Kluger describes *tabacum* in his Pulitzer Prize-winning *Ashes to Ashes*:

> Tobacco is a hard plant to love. Man-sized or taller, demanding at every stage of its growth, sticky to the touch in hot weather, highly inviting to unsightly and voracious pests, tobacco prompted one

of its more eminent growers, Thomas Jefferson, to call it "a culture productive of infinite wretchedness" in view of the hundreds of hours of backbreaking labor per acre that it required . . .

The tobacco plant is something of an anomaly of nature in that its unprotected leaves rather than its blossoms, fruit or shielded seed are what man values. . . . It has a limited life expectancy without cultivation but sprouts spectacularly when tended. If unchecked, the plant grows as high as nine feet, with wide-spreading leaves in the shape of a rounded arrowhead, sixteen to eighteen inches in length and attached to the wrist-thick stalk in an ascending spiral so that the ninth leaf overlaps the first. The leaves and stalk are covered with soft, downy hair that emits gums and aromas; these oils, resins, and waxes increase as the leaf matures and accumulate on the surface in a viscous sheen.

Tobacco originated in the Americas, in the Andes of Peru and Ecuador. Experts say it was first cultivated somewhere between 3,000 and 5,000 years ago — a few millennia before Europeans came into contact with America. Tobacco spread north until it was cultivated throughout North America and south until it was cultivated throughout South America. It was the most common trade item in the Americas.

The Native Americans figured out just about every imaginable way to use tobacco. They made tea from it and drank the tea sometimes through their mouths and sometimes through their noses. Yes: through their noses. They made snuff and chewing tobacco. They made it into enemas. They figured out how to smoke it as cigars and with pipes. They even made a primitive cigarette, wrapping tobacco in cornhusk or stuffing it into a hollow reed.

Generally speaking, South and Central Americans smoked cigars and cigarettes while North Americans smoked pipes. Although it varied by region and is hard to generalize about, most native North Americans did not use tobacco all day. They did not smoke like modern Americans. They used it in ceremonies that declared war and declared peace. They used it when the tribe had an important decision. (Again, there are exceptions.) "Crucial to the Sacred Pipe is its function as a means to offer smoke to sacred beings," says *Offering Smoke: The Sacred Pipe and Native American Religion*, which goes on to note, "Basic to the ceremonial use of the Sacred Pipe is that it is passed among the participants: it creates social communion; it joins all into a sacred circle." Common to most pipe-smoking rituals are the acknowledgment of the sky, the earth and the four directions as the source of blessings. As the website Native Americans Online eloquently describes one typical ceremony,

> Eagle Man begins a pipe ceremony by beseeching the west power, while thinking about the life-giving rains and the ever-present spirit world. Next, he beseeches the north power, the source of endurance, strength, truthfulness, and honesty, which are qualities needed to walk down a good path in life. Then, he will look to the east power. The east is where the sun rises, and the sun brings us knowledge, the essence of spirituality. Without knowledge, we become ignorant and cause harm to ourselves and others. The fourth energy is the south power, which brings us bounty, medicine, and growth. Next to be acknowledged is the earth spirit. Eagle Man touches the pipe to the ground, and says, "Mother Earth, I seek to protect you." Since Mother Earth depends on the sun's life giving energy, the pipe is then held up towards the sky. Lastly, the pipe is held straight up to the Great Spirit, the Great Mystery, the unexplainable source of all life. These words are then spoken: "Oh Great Spirit, I thank you for the six powers of the universe." Unlike many westerners,

Eagle Man explains that the person reaching out to the spirit world has no fear: "Most of us are not afraid of the Great Spirit. We don't fear something that has given us our life."

It is unimaginable for a Native American to break his word after smoking the sacred pipe in the pipe ceremony. In the past, the signing of treaties was always accompanied by pipe ceremonies because Indians believed that smoking the pipe would secure the arrangement. No one would be foolish enough to lie or go back on their word once the pipe was smoked because the pipe was the vehicle for carrying their word up to the Creator. And in return, a blessing would descend from the Creator to the individuals smoking it.

Iain Gately is also eloquent when he describes the personal use of tobacco by Native Americans in his book *Tobacco: A Cultural History of How an Exotic Plant Seduced Civilization*. There were the big pipes, used by a gathering of the tribe, and there were smaller pipes.

These pipes were for personal use: when an individual wished to communicate with his totem, or the spirit world, he would smoke his tobacco pipe, which had been shaped to represent his totemic animal or a recognized messenger with the spirits. Smoking appears to have been a form of profound meditation — a device to raise the smoker above the distractions of a world of flesh. As a smoker inhaled he literally drank the substance of the eternal, and the smoke he exhaled in turn represented his questions or desires transubstantiated into a form acceptable to the spirits. As soon as he lit his pipe, the smoker would exhale in the four cardinal directions — north, south, east then west — in order to orientate his prayers towards their intended recipients.

My Native American friend Kevin tells me that it is still traditional among some natives to offer a gift of tobacco to the shaman before asking your questions.

Tobacco spread throughout the Americas. Everyone smoked it and grew it and traded it. Its importance is hard to deny. It is important to realize: long before Europeans arrived, tobacco totally penetrated Native American society. Tobacco was to be taken seriously as a commodity.

When Europeans got to the Americas, it did not take them long to catch on to tobacco. They observed how Native Americans traded it, grew it and used it in ceremonies and as part of their medicine. They observed this use and took some back to Europe, starting a second process of growth for tobacco — first the Americas, then the rest of the world — that has not ceased to this day.

So those are the most basic facts of tobacco.

Smoking takes a little longer to explain.

4.

I am a smoker.

Technically what this means is that several times a day or more I inhale the smoke of the burnt leaves of a plant of the genus *Nicotiana*, mostly *tabacum* (probably) and maybe some *rustica* — it depends on the blend. I do this in the form of a cigarette — a "class A" cigarette.

(Like most smokers, I was mystified as to what a "class A" cigarette was, though it figured prominently on the pack. I figured vaguely that it probably had something to do with the quality of the tobacco — and in this I was wrong. As it turns out, it refers to dimensions. A class A cigarette is one that weighs less than three pounds per thousand. A "class B" cigarette, on the other hand, refers to cigarettes that weigh more than three pounds per thousand. A class B cigarette is pretty big — as much as six inches long — which is probably why almost no one produces them.)

Tobacco smoke made me sick the first few times I inhaled it. It makes one wonder why I was motivated to repeat the experience. Why, after all, do people smoke cigarettes? While there is a certain romantic conception of smoking, let me tell you there is nothing romantic about coughing up phlegm at six in the morning and then still reaching for that first morning cigarette. Certainly there is nothing cool about smelling like an ashtray. No, I have never bought into the romantic theory, the coolness theory of smoking. It may look cool if you've never tried any, but once you have tried some, that illusion goes away. The easiest answer to why people smoke and probably the most accurate one is: because of the nicotine. Without getting really technical, we can sum it up by saying that it stimulates the parts of the brain that make you feel pleasure, the so-called "reward pathways." Nicotine does this by increasing the level of the chemical dopamine, which is frequently associated with this feeling of pleasure. Each time you inhale a puff of cigarette smoke, the nicotine reaches your brain in about 7 to 10 seconds. Since people tend to take about 10 drags on a cigarette in the 5 minutes it takes most people to smoke a cigarette, and since smokers usually smoke about 30 cigarettes a day, that means you're getting about 300 hits of pleasure a day. That's a powerful reinforcer. Since the effects wear off a few minutes later, pretty soon you want another cigarette, and so the cycle repeats itself over and over throughout the day.

Nicotine is powerful — much more powerful than most people realize. How many smokes before you're hooked? It has been shown that even if you smoke as few as four cigarettes as a teenager — just four cigarettes — they probably have you for life. As the eminent psychologist Michael Russell wrote, "Over 90% of teenagers who smoke 3–4 cigarettes are trapped into a career of regular smoking which typically lasts for some 30–40 years." According to a 2012 surgeon general's report on smoking and youth, "Nearly all tobacco use begins in childhood and adolescence. In all, 88% of adult cigarette smokers who smoke daily report that they started smoking by the age of 18." There's a reason they used to advertise cigarettes to children. Once you've got them, they'll be your customers for a very long time indeed.

*

I have been smoking more or less continually since I was twelve years old. I am now in my mid-forties. This means I have been smoking more than thirty years. To give some perspective on that number, it means I have been smoking for about three-quarters of my life or about ten times as long as my longest romantic relationship. It is long enough to have gone to a four-year college eight times.

I smoke about a carton every five days, which works out conveniently to about two packs a day. Most days I smoke less but on Mondays I go out at night — pool league — and smoke more. This happens when I am having a couple of beers with the boys.

These days I smoke a cheap brand from India and pay about $4.50 a pack. This is to say that cigarettes are expensive, even the cheap ones. How much do I pay in a month? In 30 days? That's about $270.

Two hundred seventy dollars? Are you kidding me?

Do you think I am rich?

To give some perspective on that number, two hundred seventy dollars is enough to make a car payment. Not a stripped-down car, the base model — no, a fairly nice car.

That I am willing to devote this much of my income to smoking says something.

*

Addiction.

According to *Psychology Today* in their article "What Is Addiction?":

SMOKING

Addiction is a condition that results when a person ingests a substance (alcohol, cocaine, nicotine) or engages in an activity (gambling) that can be pleasurable but the continued use of which becomes compulsive and interferes with ordinary life responsibilities, such as work or relationships, or health. Users may not be aware that their behavior is out of control and causing problems for themselves and others.

When I started smoking, a twelve- or thirteen-year-old could walk into a corner store and buy butts. If anyone questioned you, you just said, "They're for my dad." No one worried about it. People just didn't think about it. If anyone did give you trouble about buying cigarettes, you could just go find a vending machine. They were all over the place.

Exactly the way that I don't think about it now, about how much I smoke. I am smoking almost forty cigarettes a day without even thinking about it.

I would suggest that numbers like 270 dollars and 40 cigarettes is *behavior out of control and causing problems for themselves and others.*

There is, as they say, something wrong with this picture.

5.

The first Europeans to see tobacco didn't realize they were looking at anything special.

When Columbus first touched land in the Americas, his first contact with Native Americans was in the Bahamas; they brought him gifts of fruit, wooden spears and some dried tobacco leaves. Columbus's crew ate the fruit. No one knows what they did with the spears. They waited long enough to sail away before they threw the tobacco — a bunch of dry, useless leaves — into the ocean.

Rodrigo de Jerez, one of Columbus's crew, is given the dubious distinction of being the first European smoker. He started smoking after observing the natives of Cuba, who wrapped dried tobacco in either palm or maize leaves and, in the curious phrase of the time, "drank" the smoke. Jerez picked up the habit and brought it back to Europe, thus becoming the first person to smoke outside the Americas. When he finally returned to his hometown, his neighbors saw the smoke coming out of his mouth and nose and it so alarmed them that he was reported to the Inquisition, by whom he was imprisoned for either 3 or 7 years, depending on what source you believe.

It's hard to say exactly when smoking caught on in Europe, since it started gradually with a few returning sailors here and there, but it's known that the Spaniards and Portuguese brought tobacco seeds home by the 1550s, only fifty to sixty years after Columbus had reached the Americas in 1492.

In the Americas, Spaniards had first observed Native Americans using tobacco not only for smoking but as a medicine. According to "Ritual Smoking in Central America" in *Smoke*, a richly illustrated collection of essays on smoking in all its forms, "When the Spaniards arrived in Yucatán, they found a rich medical lore among the Mayas. The Mayas believed that supernatural forces set ailments as a punishment for their sins, and it was to the gods that they prayed for a cure. For the Mayas, religion and medicine, priest and physicians were inseparable." Although most Mayan medical lore is lost, there are still a couple of manuscripts that exist in copies from the eighteenth century, including the *Princeton Codex* (or *Ritual of the Bacabs*), which contain prescriptions for using tobacco for toothaches, chills, lung, kidney diseases, eye diseases, eruptions, fever, seizures, and so forth. Another Mayan treatise that still exists is *Yerbas hechicerías del Yucatán* (or *Herbs and Magic Spells of Yucatán*), in which tobacco, and in particular its green leaves, is "the ingredient in various concoctions for such maladies as lack of strength, pain in the bones, snakebite, abdominal pains, pain in the heart, recurring chills, convulsions, loss of speech, sore eye, buboes, various kinds of pox, and retention of urine." It was also supposed to be good for preventing miscarriages when smeared on the abdomen with some lime.

Tobacco was initially thought of as a medicine in Europe as well as in America. As *Smoke* tells us in "The Pleasures and Perils of Smoking in Early Modern England," the medical thinking in England at the time was based on the theory of humoralism, a theory concocted by the ancient Greeks and later refined by the Greek-Roman physician Galen. This rather strange theory held that the body contained four fluids, called humors, whose balance or imbalance led to different temperaments and conditions of health. The specific humors were black bile, yellow bile, blood, and phlegm, but what is important about them is that they were hot, cold, wet and dry. This is, on the face of it, a rather bizarre theory that I couldn't get my head around until, purely by chance, I ran across this explication of it in Dava Sobel's *Galileo's Daughter*:

> According to medieval and Renaissance medical theory, each of the Earth's four elements — earth, fire, air, water — had its corresponding humor in the human body: black bile, yellow bile, blood, phlegm. These in turn denoted specific organs — spleen, liver, heart, brain — and conveyed the qualities, respectively, of dry cold, dry heat, moist heat, and moist cold.

According to *Smoke*, "Some balances . . . were better than others: cold and wet humours, associated with women, were characterized as slow, sluggish and particularly likely to bring about bad health. Smoking, exploiting the extreme and literal dry heat of fire, was accordingly understood to heat and dry the body to a state of manly vigor, driving out all manner of ills."

But I am getting a little ahead of myself. How exactly did tobacco spread in Europe? It may be worth quoting *Tobacco* at some length since it details both the medicinal and historical aspects of tobacco's spread.

> Tobacco began its European life in palace gardens where it was studied and nurtured by court physicians. This initial association with royalty greatly

helped its reputation. Courtiers were servile imitators and scrambled for cuttings to plant in their own residences. Kings were jealous of each other's novelties and their ambassadors were instructed to obtain tobacco seeds for their masters' courts. One such, Jean Nicot, sent from France to Lisbon in 1559 to arrange a marriage between the fifteen-year-old son of the Portuguese king and the sixteen-year-old daughter of Henry II of France, begged some tobacco cuttings from Damaio de Goes, the celebrated Portuguese botanist, which he raised in the gardens of the French embassy. Thus far, tobacco had been cultivated principally on account of its beauty. It flourished in European soil and spread to many gardens on the strength of its appearance alone. This had fed back into its yet untested medical reputation, thus quickening the plant's dispersal, for even if, as some skeptics claimed, it had no value as a cure, no one would object to its charming presence in their flower beds. Nicot, however, had other plans for his tobacco plants.

The Galenic doctrine, detailed above, ruled Nicot's thinking. He was looking for a way to fit tobacco into the system of hot and cold, wet and dry.

Some of the rumours concerning tobacco's reputed healing powers had highlighted its potential as a cure for cancer, and Nicot determined to put the herb to the test. When he chanced upon a Lisbon man with a tumour he treated him with an ointment made from tobacco leaves and effected a complete cure. After further and equally successful experiments, Nicot was confident enough to send plants and seeds to the Queen of France, Catherine de' Medici, whose fascination for alchemy, magic and superstition made her the perfect recipient of a novel and potent herb. Nicot also sent a letter containing testimonials of tobacco's powers and later advised that in addition to being applied externally, it might be taken as snuff. In the imitative atmosphere that prevailed in the French court, people without wounds or tumours began to take tobacco-snuff, or the "Nicotian Herb" as they called it, as a preventative, in a similar spirit to the consumption of vitamins today. They found the habit strangely compulsive, and tobacco use began to spread as quickly as the plant itself.

In Portugal meanwhile, Nicot's experiments had become the talk of Lisbon. The Papal Nuncio, Monsignor Prospero St Croce, obtained some seeds for the Pope that His Holiness instructed to be sown in the gardens of the Vatican. Tobacco also reached Italy under the auspices of Cosimo de' Medici,

Grand Duke of Tuscany and the richest man in Europe, who obtained his seeds from his relative, the Queen of France. They were entrusted to the Bishop of Saluzzo, who nurtured them in his palace. From here monks carried the seeds to other Italian kingdoms, and from thence tobacco was taken to Bohemia.

And then, as I outlined in the Introduction that begins this book, tobacco started spreading all over the place. Within about one hundred fifty years, it had spread around the globe.

6.

Addiction again.

In addition to *behavior out of control and causing problems for themselves and others*, what this means is you've got The Habit.

The Habit is there all the time. The Habit never goes away. The Habit comes first and don't you forget it.

What having The Habit means is that you always go to the store for your butts first thing in the morning or last thing at night. It means The Habit wants you to always have a supply. It means you stay away from places where you can't supply The Habit. If I can't get my dose of The Habit, I get antsy, nervous, high strung. If this goes on long enough, I start to have difficulty concentrating, I have a slight euphoria, my eyes don't seem to focus right. I get giddy. I have trouble with my short-term memory.

By its very nature, The Habit is repulsive to society. Every time you supply The Habit, you risk social disapproval.

But The Habit is more important. You indulge The Habit freely.

I have The Habit.

As of 2013 there are approximately 1.2 billion smokers on the planet. This is out of a population of 7 billion. One out of every three adults is a smoker.

All of these people have The Habit.

*

Withdrawal.

In a way you could say that you don't smoke for the pleasure of it. You smoke to avoid withdrawal.

If you don't smoke for a while — say a couple of hours — not only are you deprived of the pleasure of smoking, that first satisfying puff, that last deep inhalation, you are also subject to a variety of withdrawal symptoms, some of which I have mentioned. But there are others.

According to Leslie Iverson's "Why Do We Smoke?: The Physiology of Smoking" in the essay collection

Smoke, addiction wields a two-edged sword over its victims.

Two key characteristics are a compulsion to go on taking the drug, and a withdrawal syndrome that results in psychological and sometimes physical discomfort when the drug is withheld. The compulsion to go on taking the drug may be extremely pressing in some cases — as with some heavy tobacco smokers who wake up in the middle of the night in order to smoke a cigarette — or less so in others. The compulsion is driven by "craving" for the drug and may become so strong that it comes to dominate all other aspects of life and the drug user loses control and is unable to limit intake. On the negative side, "withdrawal" may be accompanied by severe physical discomfort that can even become life threatening. Thus, heroin addicts can suffer severe gastrointestinal pain, headaches and convulsion during withdrawal. Milder physical signs accompany withdrawal from nicotine, but the psychological distress is very real — including depressed mood, unhappiness, irritability, anxiety, frustration and difficulty in concentrating. These unpleasant psychic symptoms of nicotine withdrawal persist for long periods, during which the ex-smoker experiences intense craving.

Withdrawal, in other words, is not fun. Many people want to quit and just can't because of withdrawal. And it lasts a long time. I know that the few times I have quit, withdrawal has lasted a month or more. The intensity of it decreases, it's true, but when you are having bizarre dreams every night and can't sit down for more than a few minutes, when you practically hallucinate in your waking hours, it is not something you want to go through. Nothing prepares you for how hard it will be. *Why don't you have any willpower?* people say. *Just get through it.* Clearly they have no idea what they're talking about.

7.

When people think of slavery in the American South, they typically think of cotton. But slavery in what was to become the United States — the British colonies — started with tobacco farming.

Growing tobacco is a labor-intensive business. It occupies much of the year and requires extensive manual labor. As Jordan Goodman's exhaustively researched *Tobacco in History* lays it out:

> Tobacco cultivation in the seventeenth century absorbed about half of the year's working time. The slackest time of the year was between January and early April during which time the seedbeds were being made and tended. In these months, typically the only time in the year when workers could afford some leisure time, only about 10 per cent of available working time was used on the fledgling plants. In April, however, labour demands rose enormously. Transplanting absorbed virtually the entire working schedule in both April and May. Some respite came in June when weeds began to

appear in the fields, but in July and August topping, suckering and weeding left workers with no time for leisure. September, October and November were somewhat less demanding, but even then cutting, stripping, stemming and prizing absorbed, on average, 50 per cent of the entire working schedule.

Tobacco cultivation was often merciless with labour. The planter, as we have seen, did not escape lightly. Even if he did not work in the fields — a rare event in the Chesapeake with the possible exception of the very big landowners — his consciousness, if not his hands, was always involved in critical decisions. . . . Different kinds of skills were displayed throughout the year within an unchanging regime of extreme careful handling. The most skilled work occurred in cutting and in prizing. The cutter did not just perform an intensive task — each plant had to be cut separately and handed carefully to someone who would gather several plants at a time — but he had to make decisions in the field as to which plants to cut and precisely where to make the incision. Prizing was an activity that required considerable judgement and acquaintance with the materials. The object of prizing was literally to stuff a wooden barrel with as many layers of tobacco leaf as possible without rupturing the container. These hogsheads of tobacco were exceedingly heavy. . . . What came out of the hogsheads on the other side of the Atlantic [i.e., the quantity and quality of the tobacco] was the result not only of the curing stage but more importantly of prizing. Planters were under a strong incentive to pack the hogsheads to breaking point since freight rates were reckoned on the number not the weight of hogsheads.

Careful hands-on work was required at every stage of the process. And this is where the early Chesapeake — an area that comprises the parts of Virginia and Maryland bordering on the Chesapeake Bay, the first major American tobacco region — encountered a problem: a shortage of labor. The population of Virginia at this time — the early 1700s — could be numbered in the high tens of thousands, about a hundred thousand in fact, a population that was largely spread out over the land rather than gathered in cities: "Even as late as 1770, with a total population accounting for as much as 30 per cent of British North America, Virginia and Maryland could count only two principal towns, Norfolk and Baltimore, each of which had only 6,000 inhabitants . . ." Early colonists' response to the need for labor was to recruit indentured servants from the homeland, each of whom would serve a given number of years in return for his or her passage, after which time they would be free to start farms of their own and thus create the need for more labor.

The first nineteen slaves in English North America were brought to Jamestown, Virginia by a Dutch vessel in 1619 and were paid for with — what else? — tobacco.

The gradual replacement of indentured servants with slaves is detailed in David Brion Davis's magisterial *Inhuman Bondage: The Rise and Fall of Slavery in the New World.* The book tells us that by the time of the American Revolution, Virginia and Maryland contained not only one third of the entire country's population, but more than half of the nation's slaves. By 1775, two-fifths of Virginia's population were African slaves. This was *not* an inevitable development.

> Despite the arrival of a handful of black slaves, English indentured servants more than met the demand for labor stimulated by Virginia's great tobacco boom of the 1620s. . . . Until the last third of the seventeenth century, there were enough English teenagers, farm laborers, and artisans who were deluded by the colonizers' propaganda to meet the Chesapeake colonies' expanding demand for labor.

The flow of such voluntary immigrants was supplemented by the deportation of petty criminals, including debtors, as well as Irish prisoners and rebellious Scots.

The picture began to change dramatically when the English birthrate fell, especially during the Civil War of the 1640s, when wages rose in England, and when the city of London needed rebuilding after the disastrous fire of 1666. Moreover, many English migrants or potential migrants found such new colonies as Pennsylvania, New York, and South Carolina more promising. Thus, beginning in the mid-1670s, large landowners in Virginia and Maryland, many of whom said they would prefer white indentured servants, turned to the purchase of slaves directly from Africa. In the late 1670s white servants still outnumbered black slaves four to one, but by the early 1690s slaves outnumbered white servants nearly four to one. The slave ships would drop anchor near the houses of great planters along shores of the York, Rappahannock, or Potomac rivers. Wealthy planters, like Robert "King" Carter, who owned the local iron foundry, flour mill, and blacksmith shop, would then board a ship, examine slaves, and agree for a 10 percent commission to sell the captive Africans to his neighbors.

Or, as *Tobacco in History* puts it so succinctly, "Tobacco farms were transformed into tobacco plantations." Tobacco slavery did not just set a precedent for cotton slavery; one might say that it created the conditions for it, the culture and population for it; one might even say that it helped make cotton slavery possible.

8.

When I was fifteen-sixteen-seventeen, I would get up in the morning and head down and feed the stove. This was how we heated the house. Usually the fire was out and I had to get the whole thing going by blowing on the coals and feeding it paper to get the wood burning. While the fire was just getting started, I would light a cigarette and blow the smoke into the stove. That is how I began my day in high school.

Because anti-tobacco stories were everywhere even then, my head was full of visions of how tobacco was ravaging my body. I would lie in bed at night and imagine the cancer cells invading my lungs. I would imagine a doctor taking out my lungs and showing them to people. *This is what a smoker's lung looks like*, he would say.

Because I was a smoker I had a limited circle of friends. I knew the other kids who would sneak outside for a quick butt, the kids lined up before school and after school in the unofficial smokers' area. Stoners and deadheads predominated, with a few metal-head types rounding out the mix. There was no such thing as a

Goth back then. There were just kids who wore black and painted their faces white and black and listened to The Violent Femmes and The Cure and The Smiths. They smoked. A lot of rednecks smoked too.

Smoking was as much a bonding ritual for us as it must have been for the Native Americans. You bummed a smoke from someone and you had a connection. You shared a smoke with someone and you were friends. It was that simple.

*

Starting in high school, I smoked Brand X. I smoked Brand X for twenty-five years. I felt fine. I never had a smoker's cough. I could run up hills.

A few years ago, for economic reasons, I switched from Brand X, a premium brand, to Brand Y, a relatively cheap generic brand.

In the past couple of years I have developed a pretty bad smoker's cough. I feel short-winded a lot. I'm probably not absorbing as much nicotine from a cigarette, so I smoke even more.

A few days ago, I was in the convenience store and I saw an exceptionally low price for my old brand,

Brand X. I bought a couple of packs. Then the next day I bought a couple more.

After a couple days I noticed a strange thing. My cough had gone away.

I could breathe better. I didn't feel winded. And what was different? The brand of my cigarettes.

There is no way I am going back to Brand Y, the cheap butts I've been smoking these past few years.

So now I am smoking cigarettes that usually cost about a dollar more a pack. That's two packs a day, to make a simple estimate. Two packs are two bucks. That's thirty days. So my new smokes cost me *sixty bucks* more. Sixty bucks. We are now up to more than three hundred dollars a month. Over a month it adds up.

9.

Cigarette companies profit from selling a product that ensures the early death and suffering of many of their customers. This is undeniable.

How did cigarette companies manage to pull off the trick of getting their customers to use — and jealously defend their use of — a suicidal product? As the essay "Why Do We Smoke?: The Physiology of Smoking" describes, it basically comes down to our old friend Addiction.

> Why do people go on smoking cigarettes when the very real medical dangers of doing so are very well known? The answer is that nicotine is a powerfully addictive drug. The tobacco industry strenuously denied this fact for many years. But the intensive investigations undertaken by the former Commissioner of the US Food and Drug Administration, David Kessler, and others in the USA during the 1990s forced even the industry to admit that this was the case. These investigations showed, furthermore, that the industry had for many years systematically

manipulated the nicotine content of cigarettes by a variety of means — including even the breeding of genetically modified strains of tobacco with exceptionally high nicotine content.

None of this happened overnight, of course. There is a long history of tobacco use well before the cigarette came to the dominance it currently enjoys in the world market, a little of which we may find it useful to touch upon.

Of all the ways there are to use tobacco — snuff, pipes, cigars, chaw, cigarettes — it is impossible to say that any one was completely dominant at any one time. As *Tobacco In History: The Cultures of Dependence* describes it:

> For the most part Europeans, whether in Europe or the New World, consumed tobacco by smoking it: pipes in Northern Europe, and the corresponding colonies across the Atlantic, and the cigar in Spain, possibly Portugal and its possessions. Whether Europeans smoked pipes or cigars seemed to depend on which form of consumption they had encountered in the New World. The smoking of cigars, that is prepared tobacco leaves wrapped either in tobacco leaves or some other vegetable matter, was the preferred Amerindian form of smoking in Central and

South America while the pipe was common elsewhere.

The picture this presents is probably too simplistic. For instance, in Spain snuff was initially the preferred form of tobacco, later to be superseded by cigars and then by cigarettes, although none of these forms disappeared entirely once introduced. And in England, pipe smokers initially dominated, followed by a period of snuff-taking and then a return to pipes and the introduction of cigars. There was even a period in England when tobacco enemas grew in popularity. And this is not even to touch upon the non-European world, where pipes were common in most countries but some developed a unique form of smoking, such as India, which developed the *bidi*, or Indonesia, where most people smoke *kreteks* (clove cigarettes) to this day. It is really too simplistic to say that any one form of tobacco dominated a period. It depends not only on when you were using tobacco but where.

The one thing that can be said for certain is that once people stopped using one form of tobacco, they didn't stop using tobacco altogether; they simply switched to a different form of it.

*

So what makes a cigarette so appealing? What has en-
abled the cigarette companies to become and remain
so dominant in selling their form of tobacco?

There is the nicotine, of course. And in this case, nicotine is very important. You may get more nicotine in
the end from a pipe or cigar but they take a long time
to smoke; a cigarette can be sucked down in a couple
minutes, such as on a break from work. Drawing nicotine into one's lungs is also a factor. Smoke that enters
the lungs delivers a hit to the brain in about 7 to 10
seconds — faster even than if you injected it directly
into a vein.

There is also the factor that cigarettes are convenient.
With the invention of an equally convenient match in
the late nineteenth century, all you needed was a
smoke and a light — you could smoke anywhere, any
time. Pipes and cigars were considered things you
would ask permission to light up as they lasted a long
time; indeed, there were prescribed times and places
for smoking them. From the beginning, cigarettes were
considered suitable for lighting up in a restaurant, on
the street, in a house, at work, even in a hospital.

Another factor is a cigarette's relative cheapness. Anyone could afford cigarettes, which were sold initially in

packs of ten. Even a kid could buy cigarettes. A cigarette smoker could drag out one pack all day — and a lot of smokers did.

But if we are going to go into how cigarettes actually came to dominate the market, we are going to have to talk about a certain man and a certain machine. And that will take a little time.

10.

The letter salutes me by name and address and then begins:

Dear Dartmouth-Hitchcock patients and families:

You are invited to attend a special event at Cheshire Medical Center/Dartmouth-Hitchcock Keene.

We are proud to offer a free seminar, "Freedom from Tobacco: Made Easy!" on Thursday, June 20th from 6 to 7:30 in Central Conference Room #6 at Cheshire Medical Center/Dartmouth-Hitchcock Keene at 580 Court Street. This free seminar will help tobacco users and their families to address the reasons that keep people using (even when they don't want to) and will offer solutions to stop and stay stopped.

So. Hmmmm. It seems that my doctor is getting a little more aggressive about this "community health" thing.

It's only been in the past couple visits that I've gotten honest with my doctor about my smoking. They always ask, "And how's the SMOKING going?" and I say, "Oh, a pack a day." Lately I've been saying, "Oh, a couple packs a day." Which is honest.

> In addition to holding seminars around the Monadnock Region, the Cheshire Coalition for Tobacco-Free Communities offers special discounts on nicotine patches and gum, a monthly support group, free one-on-one counseling, as well as e-mail and phone support.

It seems that they are serious about this. Special discounts? Phone support? Free counseling?

Why not a free massage? is what I say. *How about a foot rub?*

Do I really want to quit smoking? No, not really. But I figure I'll go anyway. I'm taking a couple of friends. I mean, why not? It's bound to be worth a couple of laughs.

11.

The Bonsack machine made the modern cigarette industry possible.

Cigarettes had existed for centuries; it was one of the forms of smoking that Europeans first encountered in the Americas. As the Wikipedia article "Cigarettes" sums it all up rather neatly,

> The earliest forms of cigarettes were similar to their predecessor, the cigar. Cigarettes appear to have had antecedents in Central America around the 9th century in the form of reeds and smoking tubes. The Maya, and later the Aztecs, smoked tobacco and various psychoactive drugs in religious rituals and frequently depicted priests and deities smoking on pottery and temple engravings. The cigarette and the cigar were the most common methods of smoking in the Caribbean, Mexico and Central and South America until recent times.
>
> The South and Central American cigarette used various plant wrappers; when it was brought back

to Spain, maize wrappers were introduced, and by the 17th century, fine paper. The resulting product was called papelate and is documented in Goya's paintings *La Cometa, La Merienda en el Manzanares,* and *El juego de la pelota a pala* (18th century).

By 1830, the cigarette had crossed into France, where it received the name cigarette; and in 1845, the French state tobacco monopoly began manufacturing them.

In the English-speaking world, the use of tobacco in cigarette form became increasingly widespread during and after the Crimean War, when British soldiers began emulating their Ottoman Turkish comrades and Russian enemies, who had begun rolling and smoking tobacco in strips of old newspaper for lack of proper cigar-rolling leaf. This was helped by the development of tobaccos suitable for cigarette use, and by the development of the Egyptian cigarette export industry.

Early modern cigarettes — we're talking about the nineteenth century — were all rolled by hand. This created a problem for mass production. A skilled worker could produce about four cigarettes a minute, perhaps five. Because production was so slow, cigarette companies had to employ scores, if not hundreds, of workers. Mechanization changed all that.

In 1875, the firm of Allen & Ginter — one of the dominant firms of its time — offered a $75,000 prize for anyone who could produce a cigarette-rolling machine. A young man named James Bonsack devoted his time to creating such a machine and by 1880 had created a prototype. It was capable of rolling 200 cigarettes a minute, or about 120,000 per ten-hour shift. The machine required three people to operate.

Allen & Ginter found the machine inadequate, apparently. They never did pay the prize. It is true it was unreliable in the beginning, but this did not mean it could not be perfected.

Having the perfect machine, however, would be meaningless if you didn't have the right manufacturer. And this is where we introduce you to Buck Duke, one of the most important figures in the history of tobacco.

James "Buck" Buchanan Duke was the first modern tobacco entrepreneur. His innovations in manufacturing (using the Bonsack machine), in advertising and marketing and in corporate organization created a legacy that affects us to this day.

Duke was born in 1856. His father had started a tobacco company, W. Duke & Sons, which mostly produced chewing and cigars and pipe-smoking tobacco.
It did not produce cigarettes until 1879; at that time
cigarettes constituted less than two percent of the tobacco market. The younger Duke took control of the
company soon after and began concentrating on cigarettes, which he considered the wave of the future.
Until that time, most Americans chewed tobacco.

In 1882 there were only ten people rolling cigarettes
in Duke's factories. By 1885 he had expanded this to
700 rollers. Nevertheless, this was nothing like what it
would take to control the market. When the Bonsack
machine appeared on the horizon, Duke, unlike all the
other cigarette producers, did not hesitate to try them
out. By 1884, he had two machines. After experi-
menting to improve their performance and hiring one
of Bonsack's engineers to keep the machines in working order, all accomplished by 1886, Duke had ten machines. Since the machines were not purchased but
rented from Bonsack, Duke negotiated a favorable
contract of 20 cents per thousand cigarettes produced
versus the 30 cents all other manufacturers would have
to pay. This allowed Duke to further lower the cost of
his product below his competitors'.

If you think about it, this is a staggering number of cigarettes. If all ten Bonsack machines operated at full capacity, this meant they were producing 1,200,000 cigarettes per day. Previously, the largest factory in the country had been producing a mere 40,000 cigarettes per day.

The problem then became not one of production but of sales. And sales meant marketing. Duke proved himself a master in this area as well.

Duke used several forms of promotion that should be very familiar to us now, but that were, in fact, ahead of his time. He not only advertised on billboards and posters and in newspapers and magazines, he also gave away free samples, particularly to immigrants who might not be able to pay now, but who might return to his product later as loyal customers. He sponsored sporting events and gave away coupons in packs of cigarettes. He marketed his products with series of collectable cards — the forerunner of the whole phenomenon of baseball cards that we see to this day; in fact, the very first baseball cards were cigarette cards. Nowadays we take these kinds of promotions for granted. In his day, however, they were quite revolutionary, and with their help the company, at that time

called W. Duke, Sons and Company, captured 45% of
the cigarette market in the United States by 1889.

It's true that cigarettes at that time represented only a
small fraction of the tobacco market, but even so Duke
had captured 45% of a market with some advanced
machinery and some clever promotion. But Duke was-
n't satisfied with that. No, not by a long shot. Having
mastered production, having mastered marketing, he
pursued total dominance of the market. And not just
the market for cigarettes — for anything made with tobacco.

*

The American Tobacco Company was another of
Duke's ideas: to create a company that would consolidate
control of the tobacco market, across categories — chew,
snuff, pipe tobacco and cigarettes. Cigars, because they
have to be hand-rolled, could not be consolidated —
anyone could set up a small cigar shop. But the rest of
the market in tobacco was ripe for the picking.

An article from the Tobacco Control website with the
rather unwieldy title of "Tax, price and cigarette smoking: evidence from the tobacco documents and impli-
cations for tobacco company marketing strategies"

nevertheless rather neatly sums up the rise of Duke's American Tobacco Company. It describes how Duke used the price advantage of the Bonsack machine, of mass production, to cut the prices of his cigarettes to about half the cost of a hand-rolled cigarette, thus undercutting his competition. He then turned around and put a huge share of the company's revenue into the advertising and promotion schemes mentioned above, which gained him even more market share. Even with these expenses, the large share of the market that he captured allowed him to make a good profit. He then approached the largest remaining cigarette companies of the day — Allen & Ginter, W.S. Kimball & Company, Kinney Tobacco and Goodwin & Company, the companies that had dominated the market before Duke's rise — and more or less forced them to join into one company, to be known henceforth as the American Tobacco Company. Americans still didn't smoke many cigarettes; in 1870, before Duke's rise, the average American smoked less than one half cigarette per year, but by 1890, with Duke's low prices and heavy promotion affecting the market, that number had risen to 35 cigarettes a year.

In its first year, American Tobacco controlled 90% of the domestic *cigarette* market — only a small part of the total U.S. tobacco market, it is true, but significant.

Duke was aggressive and immediately parlayed this dominance of the cigarette market into an attempt to control the whole thing. He used the profits gained from cigarettes to subsidize moves into selling the other forms of tobacco, particularly through the use of what were then called "fighting brands": very low-priced brands, sometimes sold at a loss, that were meant to undercut other brands and drive them out of the market. As *Tobacco* describes it:

> Meanwhile, in the United States, the American Tobacco Company, the monster created by Buck Duke to corner the nation's cigarette market, was beginning to throw its weight around. Although it did not enjoy the punitive powers of European state-owned monopolies — it could not, for instance, imprison or kill its competitors — it had formidable financial muscle which it used to threaten any company or individual that stood in its way. For example, when a retailing chain attempted to sell competitors' brands they were advised by American Tobacco that unless they pushed its products alone "we would consider it in our interest to hamper your enterprise in every way we could". The retailer complied, knowing that American Tobacco could and would set up shops within sight of every one of its own outlets, selling cigars, cigarettes and

chewing tobacco at half price until the retailer went out of business.

Duke not only spread his business horizontally, absorbing different areas of the market and bringing competitors under his wing, he engaged in vertical integration as well. More and more, everything involved in the process of the production and sale of tobacco was brought into his structure and streamlined. He pursued this course with his usual ruthlessness. As detailed in *Ashes to Ashes*,

> To meld five hotly competing companies into one organization, Duke lost no time in picking the ablest employees from the collective pool and discarding the rest. No one could call that cruelty — only prudence. Similarly, American Tobacco's cigarette manufacturing was now centralized at the former Allen & Ginter factory in Richmond, closest to the source of the basic commodity and an abundant supply of labor. The Bonsack company, which had promoted the cigarette combination in order to help achieve economies of scale and a more popular and profitable product, was rewarded by having its royalty rate driven down to about one-third of its former level — but where else could Bonsack turn except abroad? Duke's distributors, too, now had

to accept a profit margin ceiling of 10 percent, like it or not, and monitor the prices fixed by the company for retailers to charge the public. Those jobbers who did so vigilantly were rewarded with a rebate, while those who failed in their oversight could now be cut sharply without fear of losing customers to waiting competitors. And the cigarette combination was big enough now to avoid competitive bidding at auction for the raw leaf; tobacco farmers, having hauled their perishable crop long distances to market, were thus often at the mercy of take-it-or-leave-it bids by American Tobacco. Against his few surviving competitors Duke employed comparatively grinding tactics, cutting prices selectively by brands and locations until the smaller independents died off or could be absorbed on the cheap.

As a result of these and other tactics, American Tobacco came to control about 80% of the total U.S. tobacco market. In 1890, the American Tobacco Company was worth $25 million. By 1910, that number had grown to $350 million. To get some idea of what that means, one 1910 dollar would be worth a little over 24 dollars now. In other words, American Tobacco was worth more than $84 billion in 2013 money.

The sheer size of the company and the kinds of tactics it engaged in probably ensured that American Tobacco would eventually come to the attention of the federal government. The reason for this scrutiny was that the American Tobacco Company was starting to look more and more like a monopoly, one of the biggest. You couldn't compete with it and, if you were involved in any way with the tobacco business, you couldn't escape it. American Tobacco more or less dictated the terms of the market to everyone else — and that made it a monopoly. At the time — suit was filed in 1907 — U.S. Steel and Standard Oil, still household names, were the two biggest companies in the United States. American Tobacco was third.

The Tobacco Control article cited above goes on to describe the monopoly's breakup into several competing companies and the broad outlines of the resulting U.S. tobacco market. In 1911, under the Sherman Antitrust Act, American Tobacco was found to be a monopoly and was broken up into four supposedly "competing" companies: American Tobacco Company (ATC), RJ Reynolds Tobacco Company (RJR), Liggett & Myers Tobacco Company (L&M), and P Lorillard Company. By 1925, three of these companies — ATC (21.2%), RJR (41.6%), and L&M (26.6%) — controlled about 90% of the cigarette market, which grew from 35 cigarettes smoked per capita in 1890 to 977 cigarettes per capita in 1930. Cigarettes were now the dominant form of tobacco used by Americans.

In a way, though, the breakup of American Tobacco didn't really lead to more competition in the market-place. It's true that the companies competed with each other for market share, but that didn't keep the prices of cigarettes down as it would for products in most other markets. Basically, the cigarette companies colluded with each other to keep prices up. Whenever one company raised the prices of its cigarettes, usually RJR, the other companies would follow suit, leading to much higher profits in the tobacco industry than in other industries. It wasn't until the Great Depression that some new, smaller companies started producing cigarettes at lower prices — the "10 cent brands" — and were able to get into the market. When all of the big companies cut their prices in response to this change in the market, it was seen as a sign of blatant collusion, leading to another conviction of violating the Sherman Antitrust Act in 1932. Eventually, two of these newer companies — Philip Morris (PM) and Brown & Williamson (B&W), a subsidiary of British American Tobacco, another of Duke's creations — would become the other two Big Tobacco companies.

These six companies — the companies we mean when we talk about Big Tobacco — were to dominate the U.S. cigarette market through the rest of the 20th century; they continue to dominate it today, in the early 21st century, and as of this time they are aggressively pursuing world markets as well. Just six companies — and five of them started with Duke.

12.

If you smoke, you smell. This is undeniable. My daughter, five years old at the time and reunited with me after an absence, told me bluntly, "You stink." I never smoked when she was around me. The only time I ever had a smoke when she was in my care was when she spent a couple hours playing on the playground I had brought her to and I sneaked one from outside the playground, all the while watching her.

But when you smoke, let's face it, you smell. The worst thing is your hands. When the skin yellows between your first and second finger, even a little, they give off an odor. The clothes you're wearing absorb some too. Your hair. Your breath smells like death, like an ashtray. There's a reason people won't date smokers. They smell.

Then there is the shit you cough up. There is phlegm, which sometimes has chunks in it. Yes: it hardens up and comes up in pieces. This is never pleasant.

I was a freshman in college when I started coughing up phlegm. I feel bad for my roommate; he was not a smoker and had to put up with my lighting up in the middle of the night. I would stay up half the night to study, chain-smoking the whole time, then in the morning I would cough up a lot of phlegm in the shower.

But what can I say? I am hopelessly addicted and I make no apologies for it. I have been so desperate for a smoke — jonesing so bad, as they call it — that I have actively contemplated stealing the butts out of the ashtray outside a convenience store. I don't think I have ever sunk that low. I have bummed cigarettes from strangers certainly — who hasn't? — but the lowest I have gone was to pick a half-smoked cigarette out of my parents' ashtray when I was a teenager, and even that says a lot.

When you are willing to compromise your dignity this badly, you really don't care if you smell.

*

Probably the only effective way to get me to quit smoking has been to meet an attractive woman who didn't smoke. This has happened a couple of times and I quit, all in all, about three and a half years. But guess what? When the girl goes, so does your resolution. And when that happens, well, you know what happens next.

SMOKING

First you bum one from a friend, thinking *Hell, it's just a cigarette. I can smoke just one.* And that's how it always starts.

13.

When people talk about the birth of advertising in the modern era, one subject always comes up: cigarettes. This is another area where Duke's influence was key. As *The Cigarette Century* has it, "One journalist in 1907 described him as 'always an aggressive advertiser, devising new and startling methods which dismayed his competitors . . . always willing to spend in advertising a proportion of his profits which seemed appalling to more conservative manufacturers.' The cigarette industry would set unprecedented rations of promotions costs in relation to sales. In 1889, for instance, Duke's American Tobacco spent $800,000 on advertising, compared to sales of $4 million to $4.5 million. In this respect — as in others — Duke anticipated central elements of twentieth-century marketing . . . Soon, billboards and buildings throughout the states carried cigarette ads, studding urban and rural landscapes with towering promotions."

Eight hundred thousand dollars is a lot of money even now, but in 1889 it was simply staggering. One dollar, just one dollar, was worth more than twenty-five of our dollars now. That means that Duke was spending at least $20,000,000 in today's money. And remember, he was just getting started. This was closer to the beginning of his career than its end. The American Tobacco Company was not nearly as big as it would become in the years ahead, after it had established its monopoly. Plus, the country was a lot smaller. You didn't have to reach nearly as many people: about 63 million, according to the 1890 census, as opposed to about 310 million in 2010. That $20 million was concentrated on about one-fifth of the population we have now — a significant difference.

The kind of spending on advertising that Duke engaged in set a precedent. He led the way down a path that cigarette companies have been following ever since. If you want to compete, you've got to keep up — and Duke set a fast pace indeed.

For instance, in 1928 alone the American Tobacco Company spent $7,000,000 on a single campaign promoting Lucky Strike cigarettes. That's about $170 million dollars now, and it was spent on a population that was only one-fifth the size of ours in the present day. And as the century progressed and the cigarette companies competed with each other for their slice of the market, their advertising budgets only grew.

The Wikipedia article "Tobacco advertising" is a trove of information. Among many other things the article details how much Big Tobacco has spent on cigarette advertising in recent years.

> The Federal Trade Commission claimed that cigarette manufacturers spent $8.24 billion on advertising and promotion in 1999, the highest amount ever at that time. The FTC later claimed that in 2005, cigarette companies spent $13.11 billion on advertising and promotion, down from $15.12 billion in 2003, but nearly double what was spent in 1998. The increase, despite restrictions on the advertising in most countries, was an attempt at appealing to a younger audience, including multi-purchase offers and giveaways such as hats and lighters, along with the more traditional store and magazine advertising.

$13.11 billion . . . $15.12 billion . . . and that was a few years ago, before China — the world's biggest cigarette market, with 350 million smokers — even opened the door to Big Tobacco. God only knows what they're spending now.

*

Cigarette advertising is not just impressive for the amounts of money involved. It also pioneered new techniques and new kinds of imagery that have since become commonplace in American culture and increasingly in the world culture at large. We have lived with these things long enough that it is easy to forget there was a time when these things were new.

Just as a demonstration of the lasting impact of cigarette advertising and design and promotion, if you went onto Amazon today and searched for "cigarette collectibles" you would be prompted with about 160 results, most of them being books dealing with cigarette lighters or cigarette cards. Cigarette cards are interesting — another of Duke's innovations. Cigarettes used to be sold in paper packaging that manufacturers stiffened with cards to keep the package from getting bent up, protecting the smokes inside. Duke's innovation was to use these cards as marketing tools. He printed them with pictures of actresses, scantily clad, or with portraits of Civil War generals. He turned them into collectibles. The first baseball cards were cigarette cards. People wanted to collect whole sets and to get them they bought his cigarettes. Like many of Duke's innovations it was deviously simple and it worked. It was also one of the first cigarette marketing efforts aimed directly at youth.

While the cigarette market grew immensely during World War I, both among a stressed-out population at home and among American soldiers to whom cigarettes were distributed as a part of their rations and who found them both a comfort in battle and a solace during the long, boring, homesick waiting in the lulls between action, a new market emerged that advertising increasingly targeted: women. Men, after all, had been using tobacco in one form or another in large numbers for centuries, but American women were a largely untapped market. To advertise to women was to attempt to overcome traditional attitudes toward women and smoking. Prior to that time, smoking simply wasn't considered ladylike. As *Ashes to Ashes* describes one famous ad,

> "Blow some my way," implored a fetching young woman nestled by her devoted companion on some idyllic crag as he puffed away in a 1926 Chesterfield ad considered daring for its day.

The book also explains that

> Just as men who smoked them had been denounced as unmanly and degenerate, so women who used cigarettes were widely perceived as unladylike and exhibitionist. In polite circles, tobacco was taken as

fit only for the "sporting girls" of the demimonde and other professional performers of their sex. Increasingly, though, women themselves came to recognize in the cigarette a far more aesthetically pleasing experience than with any other form of tobacco use, especially the cigar. The latter was long, strong, dark, thick, aromatically overwhelming, and took forever to consume. The cigarette, by contrast, was short, mild, white, lean, a fraction as smelly, did not cling ineradicably to clothing and draperies, and could be taken briefly in the interstices between the numberless tasks that made up a woman's day. But women who did so publicly continued to be stigmatized in the early years of the twentieth century as possessors of dubious character.

Within a few years, however, the social currents of modernity and the industrial age were forcing a change. While the intensifying drive for the vote was the catalyst, women came to view their degraded status in a broader context; as they had been disenfranchised from the first, so, too, had they been disembodied and dishonored by men's denial of their right to sexuality and refusal to recognize their human worth. . . . The approach of war intensified the outpouring of feminist fervor in various forms. Women were needed more in the workplace, and offices, clubs, and the new department stores drew them away from home, while the spread of the telephone, mass transit, the automobile, the phonograph, and motion pictures helped spring them from a sequestered existence defined largely by the many services they were expected to render their families.

Cigarettes, for women, were both a symbol of liberation and the liberation itself. Cigarette smoking among women at first became common, it has been noted, exclusively indoors: at home, in shops and in stores and in other environments outside the view of the wider public eye. Smoking grew into a commonplace feature on the campuses of women's colleges, hidden away in the dorms, where it might be either accepted by the administration or, alternatively, repressed: leading to expulsions or a student's being confined to campus. But the trend, as the more foresighted administrators quickly realized, was unstoppable.

Although it was not strictly advertising but rather public relations — it was exploited to serve the same purpose — there was a famous smoking event that took place during the 1929 New York City Easter parade when a group of attractive young women marched through the streets, brandishing their cigarettes, their "torches of freedom." This event was entirely staged; nothing about it was left to accident, from the pretty girls who were involved to the photographers who showed up to take the pictures that then appeared in newspapers around the country. Edward Bernays, the nephew of Sigmund Freud on two sides of the family, was the one who conceived of this event. Bernays was a pioneer of public relations who saw his role as "engineering consent" on the part of the public. In 1923, he wrote that "The counsel on public relations not only knows what news value is, but knowing it, he is in a position to make news happen." By 1928, Bernays had sufficiently refined his ideas to publish a book called *Propaganda*, which opens with a blatant declaration on how a democratic society works. "The conscious and intelligent manipulation of the organized habits and opinions of the masses is an important element in democratic society. Those who manipulate this unseen mechanism of society constitute an invisible government which is the true ruling power of our country." Engineering the smoking "event" at the Easter Parade in 1929, then, was nothing more than putting his well-publicized beliefs into practice. By creating this event, he not only saved his client the cost of paying for advertisements, he used the media itself to provide his client with the cover and credibility of what would be seem like objective news.

Advertisements were not going away, of course. The idea of cigarette ads was not only to convince the smoker that one specific brand was superior, often that it was "milder" or "smoother" or, even more blatantly skirting the health issue, as in Lucky Strike's "20,679 Physicians Say Luckies Are Less Irritating" or Lorillard's Old Gold ads proclaiming "Not a cough in a carload." The goal of advertising was also to produce a catchy line that stuck in the smoker's mind. Camel, one of the leading brands at the start of the 20th century as at its end, was particularly successful in this effort. After a brilliant teaser campaign in 1914, with ads that simply announced "The Camels are coming," which instantly drew the public's attention and helped gain Camel significant market share right out of the gate, Camel really hit pay dirt in 1921. As described in *Ashes to Ashes*,

> An outdoor advertising specialist hired early in 1921 to expand Camel's billboard presence was playing golf one day when his foursome ran out of cigarettes and sent a caddy off to replenish their supply. Awaiting his return, one of the adman's colleagues remarked that he would gladly "walk a mile for a Camel." Within weeks, in the press and on billboards coast to coast, Americans were greeted by devoted smokers telling them why "I'd Walk a Mile for a

Camel." Reynolds Tobacco spent more than $8 million on its advertising that year, among the largest outlays yet made by any company. By the following year, its profits moved past American Tobacco's to gain the industry leadership; by 1925, Camels held well over 40 percent of the burgeoning cigarette market.

People of the generation before mine will still see you smoking a Camel and say that line: "I'd walk a mile for a Camel." It is one of the most successful and enduring ad campaigns of all time.

Another of the most successful lines of its time, less well-remembered now, was one that began to appear in ads for Lucky Strike at around the same time, as Lucky Strike and Camel battled for the dominant share of the American cigarette market.

> The Lasker-Hill team truly hit its stride, though, with the sales proposition that smoking promoted slenderness, a pitch that deftly mated health concerns and female vanity. Who thought up the idea was beside the point, but the company's version of the famous campaign naturally credited George Hill [president of American Tobacco], who was being chauffeured up Fifth Avenue one day on the

way to his marble-pillared home on the Hudson in suburban Westchester when his car paused for a traffic light and he noticed a heavy woman on the corner chewing gum. Alternate versions have this rounded pedestrian wolfing down some sort of fattening refreshment, but all agree that when Hill swung his gaze to a taxicab waiting next to his car headed downtown, he noted that its passenger was a svelte woman sipping at her cigarette holder. Eureka! Already convinced without a morsel of evidence that smoking cigarettes was an effective appetite suppressant, Hill got on the phone with Lasker at the earliest possible moment, and soon thereafter the new campaign was exhorting, "Reach for a Lucky instead of a sweet."

Naturally enough, the candy industry didn't care for this ad very much, but the ensuing controversy, always a plus, probably just drew more attention to the ads. And there were plenty of them: more than $100 million went into Lucky Strike ads in the brand's first decade.

But probably the best-known ads for cigarettes are the ones created later in the century for Marlboro. Marlboro was a brand owned by Philip Morris, the smallest of the six major cigarette companies. Originally aimed at the women's market in a time when a filtered cigarette was considered effeminate, Marlboro was a more expensive brand and turned a modest profit but was never considered a serious contender in the overall market. Philip Morris decided to completely re-brand Marlboro in the 1950s. A number of innovations went into the re-branding: a more flavorful blend and a new kind of filter was used for the cigarette itself, and there was a new kind of crush-proof box with a flip top and a new red-and-white color scheme. The lettering on the box was strong and bold. On the advertising end there were innovations as well. Rather than talk about the filter, which might only remind people of smoking's possible dangers, the ads managed to avoid talking about anything at all. They were ahead of their time in the way they relied almost entirely on images, almost devoid of advertising copy, to get their message across.

And what kinds of images did the ads use? They showed the men of Marlboro Country, a land of big open skies and big open country, and came eventually to focus almost exclusively on the Marlboro Man himself, a cowboy who roamed this big country alone or in the company of his brothers, doing what all real men must do. The ads beckoned smokers to "Come to where the flavor is, come to Marlboro Country." The goal "was to tap into certain very basic human desires and fantasies," says *The Cigarette Century*.

The Marlboro cowboy suggested a mythic time, not only before the bureaucratization and urbanization of the twentieth century, but a time of simple pleasures, before the mid-century discovery that smoking brought risk and disease. Marlboro Country promised control and autonomy in a world where these were slipping away. What was so remarkable about the brand and its promotion was its precise timing and symbolism. Just as the Marlboro Man had the fortitude to face down the elements, so too would he face down anxiety about the risks of smoking. Rarely, if ever, had marketing so brilliantly combined American values, traditions, and symbols with a promotional message. The campaign . . . offered images rich in denial and escapism, in reassurance and immortality. The Marlboro cowboy would find an enduring place at the American campfire.

Marlboro gradually became the best-selling cigarette in the country and then in the world. It still holds this position as of 2013. Without the new box and its innovative advertising, none of it would have happened. You might say that the whole world is Marlboro Country now.

14.

There is an active campaign to force smokers to quit by making cigarettes so expensive that people can't afford them. This targets people like me.

A cigarette tax is a regressive tax. A regressive tax may be the same for everybody — an example is, say, one dollar per pack of cigarettes — but the impact is felt more for the person who has less money, i.e., the poorer person rather than the rich person. As *The Atlantic* website described in its article "4 Reasons Obama's Plan to Raise Tobacco Taxes Is a Bad Idea":

> Like most excise taxes, the financial burden of cigarette taxes falls to a greater degree on those with lower incomes. A widely reported study of American smokers surveyed from 2010 to 2011 found that smokers making less than $30,000 per year spend 14 percent of their income on cigarettes. In New York, home to the highest cigarette taxes in the country, cigarettes consume nearly a quarter of their income. By comparison, smokers earning more than $60,000 per year spend just 2 percent of their

income on cigarettes.

The justification for this kind of tax is the notion that smokers cost society more than other people:

> Popular perception holds that smokers impose costs on society by consuming extra medical care at public expense. This is part of what prompted the class-action lawsuits against tobacco companies in the 1990s, culminating in the Master Settlement Agreement of 1998. Yet the evidence is that smokers pay their way, both by contributing more in excise taxes and by collecting less in services in their later years — since, to put it nicely, they're not around as long to collect.

Smokers die younger than other people. They cost Medicare less. They cost Social Security less. It's that simple.

People who live a really long time are the real drains on the system. Think about it. They live ten, twenty, thirty years longer than other people, and all the time they're a drain on Social Security, drawing a monthly check. They get little ailments — nothing serious really, but it means another kind of medication, another new specialist to see every now and then. Their little ailments add up. And then, when they die, they may die of an illness just as drawn-out and expensive as whatever a smoker suffers. Everyone dies of something. Whether it's sudden and cheap, or drawn-out and costly, is purely a matter of luck.

In a way, you could say that non-smokers have an active interest in seeing more people smoke. It's more money for them.

15.

Big Tobacco has always protected its own interests, and this includes a fierce resistance to government regulation. It is hard to imagine any other product as widely used, and used as intimately with the human body, that has escaped regulation as completely as has tobacco. In 1906, when the Federal Food and Drugs Act was passed, the intent was to protect the public from contaminated food and drugs — that people should know what they were getting and that it should be safe. Among the drugs that were initially supposed to be regulated was nicotine, but the American Tobacco Company successfully lobbied members of Congress that tobacco, since it wasn't a food and it wasn't what you'd normally think of as a drug (like aspirin, for instance: intended to be taken for a beneficial effect), nicotine was removed from the list of the substances that would be regulated.

As for attempts to control or ban smoking at the local level, there had been a few scattered efforts to do so in colonial times but they all failed due to public resistance. Naturally enough there was no attempt to control tobacco in the southern colonies, where tobacco was the basis of the local economy and was frequently used as the medium of exchange, as money. Among the very few even temporarily successful attempts to regulate smoking, Massachusetts briefly passed legislation in the mid-1600s that restricted smoking or the importation of tobacco, but these laws were quickly given up. Another example, still in colonial times, was that of the colony at New Haven, Connecticut. According to an article called "History of Tobacco Regulation" that can be found at druglibrary.org,

In 1646, the General Court decreed that:

No person under the age of twenty years nor any other that hath not already accustomed himself to the use thereof, shall take any tobacko, until he hath brought a certificate under the hands of [a physician] that it is usefull for him, and also, that he hath received a license from the court for the same. . . . None shall take any tobacko, publickly in the street or any open places unless on a journey of at least ten miles.

Within three years those laws were repealed. However, it was further ordered in 1655 that:

No tobacco shall be taken in the streets, yards or aboute the howses in any plantation or farme in this jurisdiction without

dores, neere or aboute the towne, or in the meeting howse, or body of the trayne Souldiors, or any other place where they may doe mischief thereby, under the penalty of 84 pence a pipe for a time, wch is to goe to him that informs and prosecuts.

As a result of the regulation, snooping became a profitable undertaking. In the end, however, the laws were of no avail in suppressing tobacco.

By 1680, the governor of Connecticut recognized the significance of the leaf and reported that, "We have no need of Virginia's trade, most people planting so much Tobacco as they spend." Indeed, by the early 18th century, New England-grown tobacco was being produced in great enough quantity for both domestic consumption and export.

So much for the colonial era. While there was a movement in the late nineteenth century to ban smoking, particularly cigarettes — still relatively rare, confined mostly to youth in cities, and still regarded as degenerate by the wider public, as opposed to more manly forms of tobacco like chew or cigars — it was never a truly popular movement. It was only through the relentless efforts of such reformers as the singular Lucy Gaston that any changes came about. *Ashes to Ashes* describes her:

The outcry was most righteously raised by an indefatigable spinster schoolteacher from Illinois, Lucy Gaston, whose parents had been active in both the abolitionist and temperance movements and whose own strident rectitude and physical ungainliness — she bore a beardless resemblance to Abraham Lincoln — made her an easy butt of ridicule. But she was a formidable crusader.

Gaston's fervent opposition to the cigarette was empirically based, she said: her worst students had invariably been boys who stole off for a clandestine smoke and then fell prey to the habit. She concluded that the most damaging ingredient in cigarettes was not nicotine but a compound called furfural, which was formed in the combustion process from glycerine, long used as a moistening agent in tobacco products. The wasting effects of furfural led to an affliction Miss Gaston called "cigarette face," with its telltale dissipation evident to any trained observer. A still greater cause for alarm was the widespread testimonial evidence she avidly collected of immoral and heinously criminal behavior by cigarette users, from little fiends to adult murderers. There was, of course, nothing approaching a careful study of any sizable population sample that remotely suggested an objective statistical basis for this stated proneness to depravity. But she ladled out this stew of pseudo-science and evangelism at church and school meetings across the land, and soon her legions grew. They began besieging city halls and state legislatures, the National Anti-Cigarette League was established with state affiliates, and Lucy published a monthly broadside called *The Boy,* urging young fellows who suffered cigarette face and related afflictions to use a mouthwash with a weak solution of silver nitrate after every meal for three days running, eat a bland diet, and, least welcome of all, take plenty of warm baths.

In 1898, Congress pushed up taxes on the sinful cigarette 200 percent as a source of badly needed revenue to pay for the Spanish-American War; the effect was to raise the cost of a ten-for-a-nickel pack of cigarettes by 20 percent — a considerable disincentive to the poorest buyers. By the end of the century, Iowa, Tennessee, and North Dakota had outlawed the sale of cigarettes in response to lobbying by the Gastonites and their allies, and by 1901 a dozen more states were weighing a ban on the sale of cigarettes, already in serious decline.

A ban just on cigarettes, mind you, not on other tobacco products. And most Americans still chewed tobacco or smoked cigars. At the beginning of the 20th century, there were fourteen states that controlled or banned cigarette sales, but as cigarettes gained in popularity — and as states that still sold cigarettes collected higher and higher revenues from taxes — these laws were repealed. By 1927, you could buy cigarettes anywhere in the country.

And that's about it. Aside from prohibiting tobacco sales to minors, nothing more was done to regulate tobacco — about what was in it or in the smoke it produced, about what it did to you in the end, about the health claims advertisers made about it, about any of it really — for hundreds of years, not until after the surgeon general's report on smoking was released in 1964 and made it clear to anyone with even a remotely open mind that cigarettes were harmful. But even then almost nothing was done — just a few alterations in advertising and a health warning, neither of which had any appreciable effect on smoking. We'll get to that in a few chapters.

16.

It's crazy to be writing a book about smoking while smoking. It is a testament to the power of denial. Yes, these bad things happen, but I'm fine. I cough up half a lung at one point or another during the course of the day, but it's not important.

I wish my mother still smoked. I wish that she woke up every morning with an unfiltered Camel or Pall Mall between her lips while she cursed and coughed and went through her morning toilet.

I could bum smokes off her when I ran low.

We could smoke inside during the winter.

She would stop nagging me to quit. The constant flow of criticism would end. We could sit by the fire, drinks in hand — me a bourbon, her a Black Russian — and puff away. I would blow smoke rings. She would tell me stories about when she was a little girl or relate the latest gossip from work. Smoking would be a social activity rather than a solitary one.

But that's not how it is. I freeze my ass off in winter, sucking down a quick butt outside. I can no more imagine my mother having a drink and a smoke by the fire than I can imagine her joining the Marines and shipping out to fight terrorists. My mother is one of those people who crushed out her last cigarette and five minutes later was lecturing others on the beauties of not smoking. She has been like this for twenty years. It will go on until she dies or I quit smoking.

17.

Cigarettes are big business.

To get an idea of just how big a business it is, consider the fact that the U.S. economy is roughly thirteen trillion dollars a year. The cigarette economy — the money that people spend on cigarettes, just in the United States — was mostly recently estimated by the Center for Disease Control and Prevention at $80 billion a year. That's what most newspapers or online articles will tell you. But that's a figure from eight years ago — eight years in which inflation has chugged along and cigarette taxes have increased enormously, by a dollar or two a pack in most places, and of course these expenses are simply passed along to the consumer. But even going by 2005 numbers, it's a lot of money. $80 billion is a little over 1% of $13 trillion. That's what the country spends on tobacco as a percentage of GDP.

But most people don't actually spend anything on tobacco; only one in five people is a smoker. So what does the average smoker spend? The figure most frequently quoted is 14% of their income. Again, that's the average. Some places though — like if you happen to live in New York City, where cigarette taxes alone are $4.74 a pack and you might end up spending upwards of $12 for one pack of cigarettes — smoking can run you as high as 25% of your income. What do these numbers mean? Well, it's simple math. Say you're spending five dollars per pack of cigarettes; that's a very conservative estimate. Getting out my calculator, I see that if you're smoking one pack a day, that's $1,825 per year. But most people don't smoke just one pack a day; they smoke a pack and a half. That's $7.50 a day, which works out to $2,737.50 a year. As the Chicago Tribune put it, "That's more than the average American spends on clothing in a year and close to the average spending on health care, entertainment and dining out, according to federal government data on consumer expenditures." The article goes on to note that this doesn't even take other expenses — like the twenty-five or thirty percent increase in your insurance, the depreciation on a house that smells like an ashtray — into account.

One other note: you might spend five bucks on a pack of smokes, but what are the future expenses? What does that one pack of smokes cost in future medical costs, for instance? Thirty-five dollars. I'm keeping it simple. I haven't burdened you with the loss of productivity, the time off from work, the general higher cost of smokers to their employers. Just the medical costs that come from smoking one pack of cigarettes: thirty-five bucks. That pack of cigarettes might cost you five dollars today, but in the future? And medical costs are rising faster than those in the rest of the economy. Every year there's a new test, another exam with another specialist, another medication to add to the list. I really do hope you have insurance, my friend, because you're going to need it.

18.

My father died a few months ago from cancer. He was seventy-four and had smoked his whole life. (His parents weren't smokers; they lived into their nineties.) The cancer started in his lungs and metastasized to his brain, where it created pressure on a part of the brain related to speech. In the last few months of his life he could only talk in a kind of breathless, halting whisper.

I bring this up not to appeal for any kind of sympathy but simply as a statement of fact. The honest truth is — now that his death has rendered libel laws invalid — I didn't like the man; I thought he was a terrible father and it is probably to my benefit that he neglected me. But his illness indicates that I too may be in line for cancer if, as the current thinking goes, cancer is linked to your genes. If my blatant concern for myself alone shocks you, what can I say? I'm as selfish as anyone else.

Which brings us to the subject of cancer.

Of the various ways a smoker dies — cancer, emphysema, heart disease, stroke and a myriad of other causes — cancer is probably the most dreaded. It is, because it's so common, the most palpable of smokers' ailments, the one that seizes our imaginations. It is not a pretty sight to see someone eaten alive by their own body. Lung cancer is what most people think of when it comes to smoking — it is the leading cause of death in the United States for both men and women, after all — but tobacco use actually increases the risk for many different kinds of cancer, including cancers of the mouth, lips, nasal cavity (nose) and sinuses, larynx (voice box), pharynx (throat), esophagus (swallowing tube), stomach, pancreas, kidney, bladder, uterus, cervix, colon/rectum, and ovary (mucinous), as well as acute myeloid leukemia. You can find plenty of information about all of these cancers and about cancer in general online; let's stick to lung cancer for now. A decent introduction to the subject is Wikipedia's article on "Lung cancer," which says

> Lung cancer is a disease characterized by uncontrolled cell growth in tissues of the lung. If left untreated, this growth can spread beyond the lung in a process called metastasis into nearby tissue or other parts of the body. Most cancers that start in the lung, known as primary lung cancers, are carcinomas that derive from epithelial cells. The main types of lung cancer are small-cell lung carcinoma (SCLC), also called oat cell cancer, and non-small-

cell lung carcinoma (NSCLC). The most common symptoms are coughing (including coughing up blood), weight loss and shortness of breath.

The article goes on to note that

> Overall, 15% of people in the United States diagnosed with lung cancer survive five years after the diagnosis. Worldwide, lung cancer is the most common cause of cancer-related death in men and women, and is responsible for 1.38 million deaths annually, as of 2008.

Something here bears repeating: *Overall, 15% of people in the United States survive five years after diagnosis.* What does that mean? It means that 85% don't. It means that lung cancer is more or less a death sentence. You might get a reprieve, it's true, but only if you are one of the lucky few.

Okay, so those are the facts, the statistics. But what is lung cancer actually like? What is it like to watch someone actively struggling with lung cancer — to watch someone dying of it?

My mother's boyfriend — my stepfather, for all intents and purposes — happens to have a friend, Danny, who worked as a respiratory therapist for twelve years. This means he was right down in the trenches, watching the effects of smoking, in hospitals and in-home care and later in his own business. He had plenty of time to learn about cancer.

"What's it like to watch someone dying of cancer?" I asked him one night when we were all having dinner.

Danny thought about it for a minute and then said,

> Well, first of all you need to know a little about how the respiratory system works. Then I can tell you how lung disease diminishes the effectiveness of the respiratory system and how that compromises the rest of the body — in other words, what goes wrong.

> Basically, you need oxygen for all your muscles to survive. Oxygen, inhale. Carbon dioxide, exhale. You have to get in the oxygen. You have to get out the carbon dioxide. And to breathe in, you need muscles. The main thing is your diaphragm. The diaphragm creates negative pressure at the bottom of your lungs and your lungs inflate like a couple of balloons. That's why your diaphragm is so important. On the other side, there's a natural elasticity to your chest — the tension of the muscles in your ribcage, in all the muscles related to respiration — that pulls your chest shut again and squeezes the lungs and

expels the air. So that's the bigger picture of how it functions, simply put.

If a certain part of the system no longer functions or you lose the muscle tone to keep the system going, that affects the exchange of gases in the body, the oxygen and the carbon dioxide, which affects every organ.

Which brings us to cancer. Cancer is cell-driven. It destroys the healthy cells and replaces them with cancer cells. Big colonies of them — tumors. Everything in your body is made of cells. If you have cancer of the lungs, the cancer cells are destroying the integrity of your respiratory system. And these cells can spread through the lymphatic system and the blood to other organs and start colonies there. The spine. The brain. All over.

The tumors in your lungs disrupt your breathing. The bigger they get, the worse it is. Eventually this diminishes capacity, the volume of air. If you have diminished capacity, you're short of breath. You may hyperventilate. You may become cyanotic, so the fingernails and the lips are blue. That's one of the first things emergency medical personnel look at if you pass out.

If the cancer spreads to other organs, that has different effects. If it goes to your spine, for instance, a lot of times you don't realize it. You've got a backache, you get it checked out and find the cancer. Sometimes it's in the ribs. It doesn't always present itself as a problem at first. But that can kill you too. It might go to your hip, you might fall and break the hip, you're stuck in bed because you're incapacitated, and maybe because you're in pain or because you're not in the right position, you're not using your lungs right, you're shallow-breathing. You might develop pneumonia and die. The majority of patients who die after surgery, they don't die because of complications with their surgery but because of pneumonia.

My mother, her cancer spread through the thoracic cavity and went to the spine. She was in pain, but it was tolerable. She couldn't walk very far. She was a heavy smoker. After a while she coughed up blood. She would almost throw up, and up would come blood. That meant she had an open lesion. She was too old for them to operate and do anything about it. Not much pain though. Cancer doesn't always mean pain. It's just that you can't move air very well.

When organs start breaking down and certain things don't function and if you're in pain, hospice may get involved and give you morphine. That's one of the ways they make you comfortable. As a side effect of the morphine you may start breathing less and less. In my mother's case, she had emphysema as well, which made it even worse. And that kind of thing goes on for days, even a month. Sometimes it goes on for years. And eventually you just take your last breath.

So that's cancer. But what I'd really like to talk about is emphysema.

Emphysema? I had been so focused on cancer that I hadn't really been thinking about emphysema.

According to the Mayo Clinic,

Emphysema occurs when the air sacs in your lungs are gradually destroyed, making you progressively more short of breath. Emphysema is one of several diseases known collectively as chronic obstructive pulmonary disease (COPD). Smoking is the leading cause of emphysema.

As it worsens, emphysema turns the spherical air sacs — clustered like bunches of grapes — into large, irregular pockets with gaping holes in their inner walls. This reduces the surface area of the lungs and, in turn, the amount of oxygen that reaches your bloodstream.

Emphysema also slowly destroys the elastic fibers that hold open the small airways leading to the air sacs. This allows these airways to collapse when you breathe out, so the air in your lungs can't escape.

Treatment may slow the progression of emphysema, but it can't reverse the damage.

In addition to increased risk of heart disease and lung collapse due to poor lung function, here is a graphic image:

Large holes in the lungs (giant bullae). Some people with emphysema develop empty spaces in the lungs called bullae. Giant bullae can be as large as half the lung. In addition to reducing the amount of space available for the lung to expand, giant bullae can become infected and are more prone to causing a collapsed lung (pneumothorax).

If that doesn't make you think, I have no idea what will.

"Okay, so what's it like to watch someone dying of emphysema?" I asked Danny, and he said,

We called people with chronic bronchitis the blue bloaters. They don't have emphysema yet. Bronchitis is when all the tubes in the lungs constrict and the mucus builds up. The hole you're breathing through gets constricted. The mucus plugs up your alveoli, the air sacs. The mucus gets very thick and obstructive and can't move. You're blue because you're not getting enough oxygen. Your lips turn blue. Your fingernails turn blue. You're a bloater because you tend to be heavy. Eventually the mucus in the air sacs destroys them. And chronic bronchitis leads to emphysema. Combined with even moderate smoking it usually does. Not all the time. But it can.

Emphysema is when the alveoli, the little air sacs, are destroyed.

You call an emphysemic a pink puffer. A pink puffer is usually thin, they're winded all the time, they'll walk a short distance and rest. They have to consciously work their chest muscles just to get enough air. It's a labor just to breathe. In emphysema, for example, you lose the muscle elasticity in the diaphragm. In most of your respiratory muscles, really. He's bent over because he has to mechanically manipulate the diaphragm, work his muscles to get air in. They'll purse their lips when they're breathing out, just to hold back a little air and get a little more oxygen out of it. Plus they've lost a little elasticity in the ribcage so they can't get air out. Some people, three or four times a year they're in the hospital. You can't repair the damage. Often all you can do is help restore the balance of oxygen and carbon dioxide, but that's only temporary.

The exchange of gases in the body, the balance of oxygen and carbon dioxide, affects everything in your body. Not just all the organs, but the way you feel, the way you think. You might hallucinate. You might get angry. You might not understand things or be able to think clearly. You may be sensitive to the weather because humidity makes it harder to breathe. You may get ulcers in the gut.

A blue bloater can look normal, but a pink puffer is wasting away. You can see the physical change. The whole body is breaking down.

If somebody comes into the hospital and has a breathing emergency and we have to ventilate them manually, we take some arterial blood and measure the oxygen and carbon dioxide. We adjust a machine to breathe for them. That's if they're lucky. But like I said, that's just a temporary fix. In a few months they're back. Or they could be back in a few days, and they can be in and out of the hospital and rehab for a few days or for a few years, until cells start dying and their organs stop functioning.

In my opinion, I'd rather have cancer than emphysema. Emphysemics linger for years and years. They suffer. They just can't breathe. Their quality of life has changed drastically. A lot of emphysemics I saw, the highlight of their day was to get up and be able to defecate and make it back to bed. That's the quality of their life. You're exhausted from working to move air.

Eventually the gas exchange gets so bad that there's no oxygen or you're not getting rid of carbon dioxide. The cells in your body break down and die. You turn this ashen color as you get closer to the end of your journey. End stages is just like any other disease that kills you. Near the end you just can't breathe and you panic. Absolute fear. And it's irreversible.

What can we do about it, about smoking? There's this gap in people's thinking. What people don't realize is that between the time you realize you're sick and the time you die, there's a lot of suffering. If you could really imagine what's going to happen, if you could see the real and inevitable quality of life you're going to have, you might quit. Most people make the leap from being short of breath and coughing to 'I'm going to die of something anyway, so who cares?' What they don't see is that five or ten or fifteen years of suffering in between — the debilitation, the lack of independence, the long slow drawn-out suffering. They don't think about the depression from not being able to do anything, of being dependent on everything and everyone else. If they could see that — if they really took the time to think about it and really understand what that means — it might make all the difference.

19.

Why did it take so long for the public to realize that cigarette smoking causes cancer?

There are a number of reasons. First, cigarette smoking didn't really start catching on as the dominant form of tobacco use until after 1900. That is to say, it is only in the past hundred years or so that cigarette smoking became common. Second, it takes a long time for cigarette smoking to cause noticeable problems — typically twenty-five years at least. Thus, even after people started smoking cigarettes, it took a few decades for the problem of lung cancer to start showing up in the kind of numbers that we find so familiar now. As a result, people simply didn't connect smoking with lung cancer. It wasn't obvious. As one researcher noted, "cigarette smoking was such a normal thing and had been for such a long time that it was difficult to think it could be associated with any disease." And third, when proof did start to emerge, the cigarette industry did its utmost to confuse the issue, to keep people from realizing that smoking *definitely* led to cancer and other health problems.

Some people had long suspected that smoking caused problems, but the research to prove it didn't emerge until the 1950s, when researchers in the United States and England almost simultaneously published two striking and innovative reports on the statistical link between smoking and cancer. Starting in 1953, when these reports came out, the scientific literature and increasingly the popular press began to talk about the problem. For the first time, the cigarette industry's future was threatened by a real link between smoking and illness. After all, given this new information, would people who had previously smoked start to quit? And would the industry be able to attract new smokers?

In the face of this crisis, the tobacco industry decided something had to be done — not about the dangers of cigarettes; hell no. About public perception.

For the first time since the anti-trust litigation that broke up Duke's American Tobacco monopoly, the major cigarette companies got together. The presidents of the companies met and talked about what to do. And what they came up with was to make it a public relations problem. They turned to a firm called Hill & Knowlton for help.

Hill & Knowlton was a well-known public-relations company founded in 1927 and whose clients included prominent members of the steel, oil and aircraft industries. Hill & Knowlton would directly shape the tobacco industry's response to the crisis for more than a decade, putting in place strategies and techniques that profoundly affect the public to this day.

The plan Hill & Knowlton came up with was to capture the scientific debate, to turn it to their own purposes. As *The Cigarette Century* describes,

Dismissing as shortsighted the idea of mounting personal attacks on researchers or simply issuing blanket assurances of safety, they concluded instead that seizing control of the science of tobacco and health would be as important as seizing control of the media. It would be crucial to identify scientists who expressed skepticism about the link between cigarettes and cancer, those critical of statistical methods, and especially those who had offered alternative hypotheses for the cause of cancer. Hill set his staff to identifying the most vocal and visible skeptics. These people would be central to the development of an industry scientific program in step with its larger public relations goals. Hill understood that simply *denying* the harms of smoking would alienate the public. His strategy for ending the "hysteria" was to insist that there were "two sides." Just as Bernays had worked to engineer consent, so Hill would engineer "controversy." This strategy — invented by Hill in the context of his work for the tobacco industry — would ultimately become the cornerstone of a large range of efforts to distort scientific progress in the second half of the twentieth century.

The basic plan was simple: they would recruit these scientific skeptics and form an organization to be known as the Tobacco Industry Research Committee, or TIRC for short, whose research and views could then be broadcast to the public as though they were valid scientific conclusions, or, if not as conclusions *per se*, then as valid and dissenting points of view.

The scientists who were recruited for the Tobacco Industry Research Committee were, in their way, perfectly legitimate scientists. Some of them were even quite distinguished in their fields. They did not simply sell out for the industry's money. TIRC's first scientific director, for example, was one C. C. Little, a man who had devoted much of his career to the study of cancer. He had earned a doctorate at Harvard, concentrating on genetics. After graduation he joined the faculty of Harvard, and then followed this with jobs in research. At the young age of thirty-three he became the president of the University of Maine, the youngest college president in the U.S. at the time, after which he had a stint as the president of the University of Michigan. He then went to the American Society for the Control of Cancer as a managing director and founded the Jackson Laboratory, an institution which still exists and is devoted to discovering the genetic basis for the prevention, treatment and curing of human diseases. The surgeon general appointed him to the National Advisory Cancer Council in 1937, when the National Cancer Institute was founded. Dr. Little was, in other words, a scientific heavyweight.

He was also what you might call a scientific reactionary. *The Cigarette Century* sums him up beautifully.

Little's personal commitments and a priori assumptions about cancer made him the ideal proponent of the industry's singular goal of maintaining a "controversy" regarding smoking and health. His scientific beliefs about cancer corresponded directly to his belief in the importance of heredity for understanding the causes of disease. From his earliest scientific training, Little had been deeply committed to hereditarian notions of cancer and society. In 1936, as president of the American Birth Control League, he decried the "ill-advised and unsound policies of economic relief employed in the country," which he maintained would only lead to the further propagation of the unfit, and he offered gratitude to "the gentlemen who rule Italy, Japan, and Germany for demonstrating that a program of stimulating population is a program of war." Little's eugenic science was closely tied to his politics. "Our political and sociological premise in America is based on the false premise that all persons are born free and equal. This is an absolute absurdity," he wrote in 1936. "We must segregate men according to their standing." Little also became a founding director of the National Society for the Legalization of Euthanasia and the Race Betterment Congress. He vigorously defended compulsory sterilization, urging the expansion of legislation mandating such policies. "When a sink is stopped up," he wrote, "we shut off the faucet. We favor legislation to restrict the reproduction of the misfit. We should treat them as kindly and humanely as possible, but we must segregate them so that they do not perpetuate their kind."

Little sincerely and somewhat pugnaciously believed that the key to cancer — indeed, to many of humanity's problems — was in one's genes. It might look like smoking caused cancer, he said, but really it was caused by a genetic vulnerability.

Under Little's leadership, the Tobacco Industry Research Committee did fund some cancer research, yes. Just nothing that might implicate tobacco in its causation. The genetic roots of cancer were pursued while anything that might relate to smoking was ignored. TIRC funded people like Little who were predisposed to look for the causes of problems caused by smoking in almost any other area. In a way they were a lot like the small groups of well-motivated, single-issue constituencies in both political parties today that manage to get out their message and change the focus of the entire country. Every time they found a hint that something — anything at all, however remote the possibility — other than tobacco was implicated in the causation of cancer, the results were immediately trumpeted to the media by the PR team at Hill & Knowlton. By blowing up the opinions of this small group of dissenters as though they were credible, by demanding and most often receiving media coverage equal to that of the vast and overwhelming consensus of experts who agreed that smoking was hazardous, Hill & Knowlton managed to create the illusion of a controversy that didn't really exist.

It is important to realize: Hill & Knowlton did not just send out the occasional press release. This was an hour-by-hour, day-in and day-out, year-after-year effort. Every possible threat to smoking was countered. *All* opposing research was disputed, often before it was even released. Journalists and editors were courted and seduced by an ever-present barrage of Hill & Knowlton propaganda, influencing all coverage of the harms of smoking, with the result that it produced a whole different public perception of the problem.

The real goal of the Tobacco Industry Research Committee was not to try to find the truth about cancer or smoking; it was to create doubt about the link between smoking and health problems, to create controversy over the science and give Hill & Knowlton ammunition in the battle for public awareness. The real goal was to prevent any regulation of the tobacco industry or any chance of accountability in litigation. The real goal was to keep people from quitting smoking by making them doubt that smoking might hurt them. The real goal was to keep attracting new smokers by blinding them to the risks. The ultimate goal was to keep selling cigarettes. And this, through the relentless public relations efforts of Hill & Knowlton, is pretty much exactly what happened.

I'm not offended that smoking is harmful — it's just an unfortunate fact. I can accept that; and smoking, choosing to do it or not, is ultimately up to me. And with objective information, an accurate representation of the facts, I can make an informed decision.

So as I say, the facts themselves do not upset me.

What pisses me off is that they lied about it for so long.

*

What was the cigarette industry's practical response to all this controversy? That is, what did they do to make their products safer?

Well, they came up with the filter.

Bear in mind, the filter didn't actually do much. It didn't remove any substantial amount of any toxins, any carcinogens, any nicotine. It mostly just looked like it did. It turned dark when you smoked a cigarette, leading the smoker to conclude it was actually doing something. But the darkening effect was a simple chemical reaction. An industry researcher named Claude Teague noticed that if you altered the filter's pH, it would change color as you smoked. That's pretty much all it did.

This did not stop the industry from trumpeting their filters in ads. For years, ads would proclaim things like

Liggett & Myers's "Just What the Doctor Ordered" or Lorillard's "The Difference in Protection Is Priceless." And the public completely bought into it. *A filter? Seems like a good idea.* And without actually admitting that cigarettes might be harmful, the industry played on the public's idea that something harmful was being removed. A safer product, it seemed.

Not even remotely.

Even when a filter was reasonably effective, the public didn't like it. As *Ashes to Ashes* notes about one brand with a more than usually effective filter, "smokers complained that puffing on a Kent was like smoking through a mattress." The book goes on to note that to "compensate for the taste robbed from them by filters, the new brands used stronger tobaccos that yielded about as much tar and nicotine as the old unfiltered brands — a fact never noted in the industry's advertising. The filters, by and large, were merely cosmetic mouthpieces."

Even though I know filters don't really do anything, I still prefer filtered cigarettes. Why? Because it keeps you from getting little bits of tobacco in your mouth. That would be a real problem.

*

The cigarette industry did not start lobbying the government with the publication of the surgeon general's definitive report on smoking in 1964 — they had been doing that for a long time: see Chapter 15 — but as it became clearer in the 1950s and 60s that smoking was dangerous, the cigarette lobby kicked into high gear. As *The Cigarette Century* explains:

> The history of efforts to regulate the cigarette — and their relative ineffectiveness — demonstrated the power of the industry to disrupt public health, just as it had disrupted science. If the tobacco industry did not invent special interest lobbying, they raised it to a new art form in the establishment of the Tobacco Institute in 1958. Each time Congress took up the question of tobacco and public health, proposed regulations were either fully dismantled or had the not-so-ironic impact of actually favoring Big Tobacco. Following the surgeon general's findings that smoking caused lung cancer, the first required warning labels simply proclaimed: "Caution: Cigarette Smoking May Be Hazardous to Your Health." Attempts to develop public health approaches to reduce the prevalence of smoking were stymied in Congress repeatedly. Although public anxieties about the cigarette rose in the immediate aftermath of the report, by the time the Camel Man [a famous billboard] abandoned Broadway in

1966, Americans were again smoking in record numbers. Nearly half of all adults were regular smokers in the years before 1970.

How did the Tobacco Institute come to such prominence? Because the Tobacco Industry Research Committee (now called the high-sounding "Council for Tobacco Research") had outlived much of its usefulness. Everyone knew what they were going to say on any issue, all of it designed to keep the controversy over smoking alive: Dr. Little's "crucial role would be his insistence on scientific uncertainty and his perennial call for more research" on questions of smoking and health. In its own way this was still useful — the industry would still fund it, after all — but what Big Tobacco needed was something a bit more aggressive. The public was still buying cigarettes, true, but things were starting to happen in government, and the solution to that was a more powerful lobby. As *Ashes to Ashes* describes the newly invigorated Tobacco Institute, they had "some of the best lawyers, lobbyists, publicists, and scientific consultants money could buy. Their chief mission was to treat the soaring mountain of scientific evidence against their product as a mirage or a molehill and to reassure the public that eminent authorities contested the health charges, as if there were equal validity to each side' of the ongoing cigarette 'controversy.' Senator Edward

Kennedy, hardly its friend, remarked of the Tobacco Institute in 1979, 'Dollar for dollar, they're probably the most effective lobby on Capitol Hill.'"

The problem for Big Tobacco started with the publication of *Smoking and Health: Report of the Advisory Committee of the Surgeon General of the Public Health Service.* This report, authored by five smokers and five nonsmokers, all of them experts in their fields and none of whom had previously voiced an opinion on smoking, rigorously reported on their review of many thousands of documents and studies from a variety of disciplines — statistics, epidemiology, lab experiments — on the subject of smoking and health. The report took more than a year to complete and was truly exhaustive, and when it was published it left no substantive doubt in the public's mind: smoking was dangerous. And with this consensus established, the problem moved into the realm of politics: what was the government going to do about it? After all, this was an issue of public health.

When the Federal Trade Commission (or FTC), which has jurisdiction over the advertising and labeling of products, issued new regulations that required the tobacco industry to put health warnings on all cigarette packages and ads, the Tobacco Institute went to work. As *The Cigarette Century* explains:

It was inevitable that some form of warning labels would soon be required. With the FTC rules pending and laws regulating the promotion of cigarettes being proposed in up to twenty state legislatures, the tobacco industry brilliantly reversed field. The most effective strategy for derailing proposed FTC regulations, they now determined, would be to seek congressional oversight. If the industry could not avoid government action, it could ensure that the action was taken in their preferred venue: The U.S. Congress. . . . Not only did the industry have "friends" in Congress, especially — but not exclusively — from tobacco growing states, industry lawyers and lobbyists recognized that Congress would be eager to protect its own authority against an activist regulatory agency. Therefore "[t]he Policy Committee was directed to propose a form of bill for Congressional action which would preempt the field." The industry would achieve this preemption by acceding to a package label while precluding any warning in advertisements. The "concession" on a package label, the lawyers reasoned, might offer leverage in avoiding other pernicious intrusions into tobacco marketing and promotion.

By working through Congress, the cigarette industry would successfully prevent local jurisdictions from trying to regulate them, thus avoiding "the potential nightmare of diverse rules and controls among the fifty states."

Well, politicians being what they are — some of them honest, some of them not, and some of them from to-bacco-producing states where the cigarette industry and tobacco farmers could make or break a politician's career — the struggle for control of any smoking leg-islation was immediate. The Tobacco Institute's inten-sive lobbying prevailed, however, and the Federal Cigarette Labeling and Advertising Act of 1965 pre-vented any regulation of tobacco advertising for the next four years, although it did provide for a warning on cigarette packages.

And what did we get for a warning? "Cigarette Smoke May Be Hazardous to Your Health" — the key words being *may be*, as though the harms of smoking were still open to debate. No details about what to expect from smoking, about cancer and emphysema and heart dis-ease, nothing that would make people actually see the problem. And no information on what was in the smoke, about all the toxins and nicotine. Nothing to make a smoker look at the pack and say, *Holy shit, these really aren't any good for you. Maybe I should think about quitting.* The warning was the absolute minimum — just enough, in fact, for the cigarette companies to be able to claim you'd been warned and that whatever happened to you after that was your own fault. Just enough, in other words, to protect Big Tobacco from litigation. *Hey, you saw the warning — and you made the choice. Don't blame us for what happened.* Far from being hurt by it, the industry turned the warning into a way to further its own interests, to dodge responsibility for what it had done in misleading the public. That's what Congress did for Big Tobacco — a little gift to the industry to the tune of hundreds of billions of dollars. And how effective did the warnings turn out to be? They did almost nothing to decrease smoking.

20.

Times are changing for smokers. I lived in San Francisco in the late 1990s, when smoking was banned in bars. The night before the ban took effect everyone was out at the local bar, smoking their lungs out and thus disproving the whole premise of the ban, which was that people wanted a smoke-free environment. The first day of the new dispensation I went down to the bar and said to the bartender *I understand smoking is not allowed in this establishment. Do you have an ashtray?* The bartender smiled, reached under the counter and handed me one.

I doubt you could get away with that now.

I lived in New Hampshire a few years ago when the same thing happened and there we all were, out at the bar, smoking as much as we could, trying to beat the clock. For the next few days the regulars among us would light up in the bar and laugh. Not too long after that the state started fining bar owners who didn't enforce the ban. Not a couple hundred bucks, some light little slap on the wrist. Word went around that it was more like a few thousand. True or not, suddenly people weren't lighting up any more and laughing. Sure, people wanted to smoke, but they didn't want to be the one that brought down that kind of fine on the owner. And they sure didn't want to get kicked out of their favorite bar. Now people stand outside in a little fenced-in area, freezing their butts off in winter, clutching their beers and looking like a bunch of sheep getting ready for slaughter.

Pathetic.

You can still smoke in a private club in New Hampshire, which includes places like the American Legion or the Veterans of Foreign Wars or the Moose Club or the Elks Club or whatever other kind of club you've got. But even places like that are starting to change. More and more places are relegating smoking to some dingy little back room away from the main bar, away from action. The old folks who for countless years happily chain-smoked their value-priced cigarettes at the bar are getting voted out by a majority of the members, who are younger and less likely to smoke. And there's nothing at all you can do about it. The older members are just dying off — from smoking, probably, but you could argue that's their choice.

SMOKING

And Starbucks, the coffee chain, just banned smoking at its outside tables and within twenty-five feet of their establishments. When I started going out to cafés it was unimaginable not to smoke — hell, it was half the point. A café without cigarettes is like a saloon without beer.

Maybe I'm just getting old. But this country is just not what it used to be.

21.

As people began to come forward to sue the cigarette industry in the second half of the twentieth century, they encountered a nearly unbroken history of defeat for anyone who went after the tobacco companies. Big Tobacco — and Big Tobacco's lawyers — were simply too good at putting up a wall against litigation. They did this by building on their record of denying any evidence of the harms of smoking and by blaming the victim for what happened. After all, you'd been warned about the dangers. You chose to smoke; and as a result, you should bear the consequences. Big Tobacco played this for all it was worth. As late as the early 1990s, Big Tobacco never paid one penny to a plaintiff for the harms done to them by smoking, a fact that not only saved the industry money in damages, but that they did their best to announce in the media and discourage anyone else who might try. It was a tactic that paid off on every level.

It would take more than the resources of individual plaintiffs and lawyers to bring the cigarette industry to account. It would take the full resources of almost all the state governments, working in tandem — but that

ERIC COATES

would not happen for a very long time. Along the way there were a few developments that helped make that accounting possible.

*

The first real crack in the industry's argument that smoking was a voluntary risk — essentially, a free choice for which you were responsible — was the emergence of data on secondhand smoking. Americans were willing to tolerate the idea that smokers were responsible for their own actions; what they were not willing to tolerate was the idea that your actions hurt *somebody else* — the members of your family, your coworkers and friends — who couldn't get away from your smoke. You can kill yourself, the logic went, but you don't have right to kill the people around you. That was just common sense, and it had a profound effect on public thinking.

According to a page called "Secondhand Smoke" on the American Cancer Society website in 2013, secondhand smoke is responsible for numerous serious health problems among nonsmokers, including about 46,000 deaths from heart disease, about 3,400 deaths from lung cancer, worsened asthma for 1,000,000 asthmatic children, and as many as 300,000 lower respiratory tract infections in children under 18 months of age. The estimated cost of secondhand smoke in the United States, all by itself, in terms of extra medical care, sickness, and death, is more than $10,000,000,000 a year. That's the scope of the problem even now, long after the smoking's peak in the 1970s.

While these problems weren't always clear in the early years of the debate — and of course the tobacco industry disputed all of them, backing and promoting opposition research that most frequently tried to pin the blame on things like pollution — over time they built up a nasty picture. It was a picture that kept getting worse.

By the early 70s, nonprofit groups and concerned citizens had begun to work to create bans on smoking in public places. Working at the local or state level, these anti-tobacco groups were able to get around the industry's lobby, which had been so successful in controlling the entity of Congress but which was much less effective when spread out across fifty states and literally hundreds of principalities.

The tobacco industry did fight back, though. They tried, for instance to mobilize sentiment about "smokers' rights," essentially comparing smokers to an oppressed minority like those — women, homosexuals, and blacks, for instance — whose civil rights genuinely needed to be protected. As one Philip Morris executive wrote in an opinion piece called "Smokers Get a Raw Deal" which appeared in newspapers around the country,

> The basic freedoms of more than 50 million American smokers are at risk today. Tomorrow, who knows what personal behavior will become socially unacceptable, subject to restrictive laws and public ridicule? Could travel by private car make the social engineers' hot list because it is less safe than public transit? Could ice cream, cake and cookies become socially unacceptable because their consumption causes obesity? What about sky-diving, mountain climbing, skiing and contact sports? How far will we allow this to spread?

> The question all Americans must ask themselves is: can a nation that has struggled so valiantly to eliminate bias based on race, religion and sex afford to allow a fresh set of categories to encourage new forms of hostility between large groups of citizens?

> After all, discrimination is discrimination, no matter what it is based on.

But Americans weren't buying it any more; they'd heard enough from the cigarette industry. By 1990, smoking was banned on all domestic flights in the U.S. Not only were other passengers exposed to smoke, it was argued, but flight attendants were forced to deal with it day after day after day, throughout their careers. Many restaurants and workplaces had banned it on their own already. It was a change that was sweeping across America. And what is more, people actually liked it.

*

There were a couple of other developments which came about as the result of lawsuits which we should look at for a moment, as they paved the way for the Tobacco Master Settlement Agreement of 1998. The MSA was a long time coming, and there were lots of little steps along the way.

In 1983, a lawsuit was filed on behalf of a woman named Rose Cipollone, who at that time was suffering from lung cancer. She had smoked since she was sixteen. Although the suit was called simply *Cipollone v. Liggett Group, Inc.*, there were actually three defendants: Liggett & Myers, Philip Morris, and Lorillard — all of them members of Big Tobacco. Rose Cipollone had smoked cigarettes produced by all three at various times in her smoking career, usually switching brands because she thought that another brand was safer.

The Cigarette Century has an outstanding summation of what trying to sue a cigarette company was like.

> In all such suits, the industry mounted a vigorous, three-part defense. First, it presented experts, such as C. C. Little of the Tobacco Industry Research Committee (TIRC), who testified that it had not been proven that cigarettes cause lung cancer. Many of these experts were directly employed by the TIRC or were dependent on it for research funding. According to the argument they put forward, the plaintiffs could not claim that the consequences of smoking were "foreseeable" and that the companies had a legal responsibility to warn consumers and modify their product, because the cause of lung cancer remained in scientific doubt. Second, industry lawyers argued that no specific case of cancer could be conclusively linked to smoking. Given the complexities of pathological evaluation, there were always experts willing to disagree with any particular diagnosis. Third, the defense contended that the "controversy" regarding smoking and health was well-known and highly publicized; as a result, plaintiffs were well-informed of any "alleged" risks.

They had personally accepted any risks that cigarettes might possess. Advertisements and other promotions were well understood by the public to be "puffery" and thus did not constitute an implied warranty of the product. Plaintiffs who proceeded in spite of these arguments soon found themselves facing an even higher hurdle: a blizzard of briefs, motions, and other time-consuming and costly legal initiatives brought by the defendants.

In other words, not only did Big Tobacco blame you for what happened, they would probably bankrupt you and your lawyer in the process. Many lawsuits dragged on for so long that the plaintiff died before the suit was over. That's what happened to Rose Cipollone, who died in 1984. Her grieving husband went on with the case.

The biggest effects of the case on later suits were in two areas. First, Cipollone's lawyer, Marc Edell, was successful in forcing the cigarette companies to divulge a mountain of internal documents. The importance of this cannot be overstated. For the first time, the public was able to see beyond the face of innocence and denial that the cigarette companies had put on for public consumption and find out that they were well aware of the dangers of smoking back in the 1940s, long before the Surgeon General's report and long enough for them to have done something like warn the public or try to develop a safer product. The documents also revealed the companies' deliberate strategy of denial about the harms of smoking and their attempts to mislead the public.

The second important aspect of the case was the importance placed on addiction. Experts for the plaintiffs testified that nicotine was a drug, that withdrawal was extremely difficult and that Rose Cipollone kept smoking because she didn't feel she had any choice: she felt that she *had* to keep smoking. The Surgeon General, C. Everett Koop, released a new report on nicotine at the same time as the trial was taking place, declaring once and for all that nicotine was addictive. This report was admitted as evidence by the judge. Cipollone's lawyer took this one step further, using tobacco industry documents to show that the industry had done research on nicotine that indicated its addictive qualities and had deliberately chosen to suppress this information, leaving the public — and Rose Cipollone — at the mercy of nicotine.

At the end of the trial, the industry lawyers, as they usually did, tried to have the case thrown out. Judge Sarokin refused. What he wrote on the subject makes him a hero of public health.

The jury, based upon the foregoing, may reasonably conclude that 1) defendants negligently failed to conduct research when it was warranted; 2) that they made affirmative health claims which were untrue; 3) that they failed to warn of risks about which they had knowledge; 4) that they deliberately and intentionally refuted, denied, suppressed and misrepresented facts regarding the dangers of smoking; 5) that they withheld knowledge of and failed to market a safer cigarette in order to avoid any admission of liability; and 6) that they engaged in an industry wide conspiracy to accomplish all of the foregoing in callous, wanton, willful and reckless disregard for the health of consumers in an effort to maintain sales and profits. The evidence presented also permits the jury to find a tobacco industry conspiracy, vast in its scope, devious in its purpose and devastating in its results. The jury may reasonably conclude that defendants were members of and engaged in that conspiracy with full knowledge and disregard for the illness and death it would cause, and that Mrs. Cipollone was merely one of its victims.

They still lost the case in the end. Although the jury awarded $400,000 to Rose Cipollone's husband, Antonio, New Jersey law prevented him from collecting because the jury found Rose to be 80% at fault — in other words, even in the face of addiction, she had caused her own death. Later, the Third Circuit Court of Appeals went further and threw out the judgment, saying there was no way to know if Rose Cipollone had seen or believed the cigarette ads that her lawyer had argued had misled her about the dangers of smoking.

But you might say the damage had been done. The industry documents were out there and addiction was now considered a factor in the debate.

*

But why exactly is nicotine so important?

Simple: people just wouldn't smoke if it weren't for the nicotine. This is obvious to anyone with even a remotely open mind. Would you take a tube of shredded leaves, light it on fire and suck the smoke into your lungs thirty times a day or more, especially if it was shown to kill you, if you weren't getting something else out of it? Why would you take that risk? As one tobacco industry executive explained candidly in 1971, long before the public understood the reality of nicotine addiction,

> The cigarette should be conceived not as a product but as a package. The product is nicotine . . . Think of the cigarette pack as a storage container

for a day's supply of nicotine . . . Think of a cigarette as a dispenser for a dose unit of nicotine. Think of a puff of smoke as the vehicle of nicotine . . . Smoke is beyond question the most optimised vehicle of nicotine and the cigarette the most optimized dispenser of smoke.

Or, as one member of Philip Morris's research and development team wrote even earlier, in 1969,

> the primary motivation for smoking is to obtain the pharmacological effect of nicotine. In the past, we at R&D have said that we're not in the cigarette business, we're in the smoke business. It might be more pointed to observe that the cigarette is the vehicle of smoke, smoke is the vehicle of nicotine, and nicotine is the agent of a pleasurable body response.

(And why would a tobacco company need a research and development team at all? Isn't tobacco just tobacco? Isn't a cigarette just a cigarette? You probably don't even need one — unless, that is, you are up to something.)

In the early 1990s, the Food and Drug Administration, or FDA for short, finally started looking into the idea of regulating nicotine as a drug. At this point there was no regulation at all. David Kessler, the FDA commissioner at the time, wrote about the excruciating process of extracting information about nicotine addiction from the industry's own secret files or with the help of industry whistleblowers in an intriguing book called *A Question of Intent: A Great American Battle with a Deadly Industry*. If nothing else, this book will give you an education on what a determined and well-funded minority can do to influence Congress.

One of the first real clues Kessler found about the industry's manipulation of nicotine was the remarkable consistency of nicotine levels in the cigarettes of any one brand. This is not a naturally occurring phenomenon. "I discovered that nicotine levels in tobacco plants vary not only from breed to breed, but also from one plant to the next. Even within a single plant, the leaf, stems, and ribs yield varying nicotine levels, depending on numerous factors. For example, the higher up a leaf is on the stalk, the greater its nicotine concentration." And yet, when tested in a lab, one cigarette of a given brand was found to have much the same level of nicotine as any other, despite this natural variation. "This was amazing for an agricultural product. With its vast experience in prescription drug analysis, St. Louis pointed out that tobacco companies had achieved a level of uniformity using a heterogeneous crop that matched or exceeded what drug companies, using well-defined chemical entities, could achieve. Such consistency did not happen by accident."

The next clue came from reports of testing with lab rats. As a confidential informant told him, rats were given a choice between two levers in their cages, one of which gave them a dose of nicotine while the other gave them a placebo of saline solution. What they found was that "after a few preliminary tries, the rats ignored the placebo and invariably chose the nicotine dispenser. Over several days, the animals conditioned themselves to self-administer almost ninety doses of nicotine in a twenty-four hour period. The experiments showed that the self-administration was controlled, at least in part, by nicotine levels in the blood or tissue."

The next big clue about what the industry knew about nicotine came from low-tar cigarettes. Low-tar cigarettes had been one of the industry's responses to the public's concern about health — one of several ways the industry played on those health concerns without ever admitting there was anything wrong — and these cigarettes had been heavily promoted. Since tar and nicotine tend to travel together, a low-tar or a "light" cigarette, using normal tobacco plants, would tend to have lower nicotine levels than other cigarettes. But this was not found to be so. Tests consistently showed that the low-tar cigarettes the companies were putting out actually had more nicotine than regular cigarettes. What was going on here?

It turned out that the cigarette companies were not only blending different tobaccos to achieve their target nicotine levels, they were going so far as to cross-breed plants with the goal of higher nicotine yields in mind. And that wasn't all. One member of Big Tobacco, Brown & Williamson, had actually gone so far as to genetically engineer a particularly potent breed of tobacco. Typically, tobacco has about 2.5–3% nicotine. The breed they created — it was called Y-1 — had as high as 8% nicotine. Y-1 was rocket fuel for a smoker. Blended with other tobaccos, it kept nicotine levels just where the company wanted. And they didn't just use it for research, as they initially claimed; they had millions and millions of pounds of the stuff.

Even that wasn't all. As the former industry researcher Dr. Jeffrey Wigand revealed to Kessler, cigarette companies including Brown & Williamson, Philip Morris and R. J. Reynolds had pioneered the use of ammonia in cigarettes. Yes, that's *ammonia*, the cleaning agent — the stuff that makes you rear back in pain if you happen to sniff the air a little too close to it. And why did they use ammonia in butts? Because it increased the rate at which nicotine was absorbed in the bloodstream. They knew exactly what they were doing. An industry document revealed its purpose. "Ammonia, when added to a tobacco blend, reacts with the indigenous nicotine salts and liberates free nicotine. . . . the ratio of extractable nicotine to bound nicotine in the smoke may be altered in favor of extractable nicotine. . . . extractable nicotine contributes to impact in cigarette smoke." Think you've never free-based a drug? If you've smoked a cigarette, there's a good chance you've free-based nicotine.

In boosting nicotine, the industry knew that it was manipulating the smoker. In a memo addressing what they called the "effect," one researcher wrote, bluntly comparing smokers to lab rats, that

> The effect of that smoking act upon his person is the reward. That effect reinforces the smoking act. He comes to push the lever ten to sixty times per day. Our task is to understand the reinforcing mechanism, or process, whereby the habit is established and maintained.

Or, as another industry memo sums it up, "the tobacco industry may be thought of as being a specialized, highly ritualized and stylized segment of the pharmaceutical industry. Tobacco products uniquely contain and deliver nicotine, a potent drug with a variety of physiological effects."

Just how loud is the call of nicotine? As David Kessler summed it up, "After surgery for lung cancer, nearly 50 percent of those who survive resume smoking. Even when a smoker's larynx is removed, 40 percent start smoking again."

It's true that you feel a little better if you smoke. More important, though, is that you feel a lot worse if you don't. Addiction is the ultimate carrot-and-stick enforcer. You don't even have to do anything to smokers; their bodies do it to them. All you have to do is turn them on to it — get them started with, say, three or four butts as an adolescent — and let the drug do the rest. It's simple, really. You might even call it efficient.

And the cigarette industry knew about it for a long time. As one Philip Morris executive said, "We all know it's addictive. I'd shove it in my vein if I could."

*

The Tobacco Master Settlement Agreement, or MSA for short, was the brainchild of a lawyer named Mike Lewis who had the idea one day of making Big Tobacco pay to clean up its own mess. This idea struck him after a visit to his secretary's mother, who was then dying of lung cancer; her insurance had run out, leaving the State of Mississippi and Medicaid to pay her remaining medical expenses — more than a million dollars. The cigarette companies had created this problem, he reasoned. Why shouldn't they pay for it as well?

Lewis took this idea to the state's Attorney General, Michael Moore, an old friend of his from the University of Mississippi Law School. Moore liked the idea. After consulting with other attorneys, many of whom were liability lawyers only too eager to go into partnership with the state and take a shot at Big Tobacco, Mississippi filed suit against the Big Tobacco companies and the wholesalers, trade associations, and PR firms that worked with them.

Key to Mississippi's strategy was that the suit sought damages to the *state*, not to individual smokers. Whereas in previous suits industry lawyers could point at an individual smoker and say that the consequences of smoking were their own fault, you could not apply that thinking to a broad class of people or to the expenses borne by a whole state. As the lawyer Don Barrett said, "The State of Mississippi has never smoked a cigarette."

Things heated up for the industry when other states began to get involved. It was probably the prospect of being sued by so many separate states in so many separate cases — more than thirty of them at the time — that brought Big Tobacco to the negotiating table. After all, they might win some of the cases — they might even win most of them — but sooner or later they were going to lose, and then things would become a nightmare.

In their first attempt at a settlement, the cigarette companies and the attorneys general agreed that the companies would pay $365.5 billion to the states over twenty-five years. The companies would submit to the regulation of nicotine by the Food and Drug Administration — something they had been able to avoid since the FDA was created in 1906 — if youth smoking did not decrease. They would submit to stronger warning labels and restrictions on advertising, particularly in advertising to youth. On their end, the companies would receive immunity from class-action lawsuits and there would be a limit to their litigation costs. The agreement would have to be submitted to Congress, whose approval was required for some of the conditions, such as FDA regulation.

What killed the agreement was what happened in Congress. Senator John McCain actually worked to strengthen the bill, raising Big Tobacco's payments to more than $500 billion, raising taxes on tobacco, ensuring FDA regulation of nicotine under any circumstances, and putting in place programs to prevent youth smoking. The industry would still receive immunity from litigation.

This legislation was attacked from all sides. The tobacco industry reversed course and lobbied against it intensively, spending more than $35 million on lobbying and an additional $40 million on ads opposing the legislation, saying that it was just a tax hike and that it would create a black market in cigarettes. Anti-tobacco forces hated the bill because it gave the industry immunity from litigation and, by regulating nicotine, made it a legitimate industry. They simply couldn't accept that an industry they had fought so hard against for so long would, in the end, be saved from destruction by this kind of compromise. To them, making a deal with Big Tobacco wasn't some kind of justice; it was a way of actually saving them from long-overdue destruction. Regulating nicotine made it legitimate. Immunity from litigation protected the industry. And with opposition on all sides, the legislation wasn't able to pass.

In the end, the tobacco companies went back to the states for a new set of negotiations. The state cases, after all, were still pending, and it was in the companies' best interest to reach a settlement. This time they negotiated with just eight attorneys general, resulting in an agreement for $200 billion to be paid to the states and what were regarded as modest provisions regarding marketing and advertising. Once an agreement was reached, the two sides offered the other states only a week to decide what to do, whether to join in the agreement or not, and essentially forcing them to take the money or lose it. Rather than take a chance with the courts or be criticized for turning down billions of dollars, the other attorneys general took the deal. Forty-six states were eventually party to the agreement; the other four — Texas, Mississippi, Minnesota and Florida — had already reached agreements of their own.

And what was lost? Anything that Congress had to approve of. No regulation of nicotine, for instance. Furthermore, no restrictions on marketing or enforcement on sales to youth. It only required payments of $206 billion over twenty-five years, some restrictions on advertising like the elimination of cartoons (Joe Camel, in particular, had been blatantly aimed at children) and the funding of a national program to reduce smoking.

And what else did we lose? The industry still got immunity from any government litigation. You can still file an individual or class-action lawsuit, but the government — state or local — can't ever sue them again.

*

So how did the Master Settlement Agreement work out for everyone?

Well, Big Tobacco's doing just fine. The payments to the states are covered by the price increases they've passed along to consumers. Stock prices are up overall and profits look healthy. It's true they aren't selling as many cigarettes in America as they used to, but they're more than making up for that in other markets around the world. And America, however it may be changing, is still a pretty profitable market.

As for how the states are doing, well, things could be better. As *The Cigarette Century* says,

> For one thing, there were no guarantees that the money paid by the companies to the states would go to anti-tobacco programs. In many states it became clear that the funds would simply be a windfall to governors and legislators with little interest in battling tobacco. The money itself, moreover, was inadequate to cover the costs of smoking-related

disease. In California, for example, UCSF health economist Dorothy Rice estimated the cost for just one year at $8.7 billion, but the state was to receive just $500 million. "It's a terrible deal," she concluded.

From this year — April 24, 2013 — the Associated Press reported that my home state, New Hampshire, would be getting almost $15 million more from Big Tobacco than it usually does. According to the Attorney General, we normally get about $42 million, but this year we're getting $57.3 million. That's a lot of scratch for a pretty small state. Does the state plan to use the money for anti-tobacco education? Plans to prevent youth smoking, which is where it all starts? After all, that's what the settlement was supposed to cover. Well, I'm afraid not. The state plans to use the money to deal with a routine budget shortfall.

As for cigarette marketing and advertising, it's not clear just yet how the tobacco industry has changed its practices. They can't do billboards any more, but signs up to fourteen feet wide are still legal. They've vastly increased their marketing budgets. According to a statement by Matthew Myers of the Campaign for Tobacco-Free Kids,

SMOKING

On March 13, 2001, the Federal Trade Commission released a report showing that, contrary to their claims of change, the tobacco companies spent more than ever before to market their products in 1999, the first year after the state tobacco settlement. In 1999, cigarette manufacturers spent a record $8.24 billion on advertising and promotion, an increase of $1.51 billion or 22.3 percent from 1998. That amounts to $22.5 million a day. Much of that increase was in categories that appeal to kids, including shelf displays, two-for-one promotions that reduce cigarette prices, giveaways such as hats and lighters, store advertising and magazine advertising.

The industry agreed a long time ago to stop making health claims in their advertising, but as recently as this year in Vermont, the state next to mine, Big Tobacco was once again found guilty of violating that agreement. As the reporter Hilary Niles wrote for vtdigger.org, an independent publication that covers Vermont, the state next to mine,

R. J. Reynolds Tobacco Co. has been ordered to pay the state of Vermont $8.328 million in civil penalties for deceptive advertising of its nontraditional Eclipse cigarette between 2000 and 2007.

Both parties have 30 days from the date of the ruling to appeal, and no money would be due while an appeal is pending. If the fine is paid, it will go into the state's General Fund.

The money's going into the state's General Fund? Of course! What else would you do with tobacco money?

And what exactly was Reynolds guilty of?

"The best choice for smokers worried about their health is to quit," one ad read. "The next best choice is to switch to Eclipse." Other marketing messages included claims that smoking Eclipse — because it "primarily heats rather than burns tobacco" — produces less toxic smoke than other cigarettes. That "may present less risk of cancer, chronic bronchitis, and possibly emphysema," according to Reynolds' ads.

Such unsubstantiated claims violate Vermont's consumer protection laws and the state's 1998 consent decree pursuant to the Master Settlement Agreement. That 46-state settlement, in addition to mandating the country's four largest tobacco companies pay billions of dollars in compensation to states for treating tobacco-related illnesses, imposed restrictions on their promotional practices.

Even after the MSA and a March 28, 2005, letter from 40 state attorneys general demanding that Reynolds discontinue its deceptive advertising of Eclipse, the company persisted. The state of Vermont filed suit against the company that summer.

And one last thing: as many observers have pointed out, the states are now essentially the partners of the tobacco industry. The states depend on cigarettes to keep that money coming in — not just in taxes as always, but now in the form of the yearly payments from Big Tobacco. The states have a clear and vested interest in Big Tobacco's future. Is that really where we wanted to end up?

22.

So I went to the hospital's smoking cessation seminar. In lieu of any genuine desire to quit myself, I shanghaied a couple of my friends into going with me. If I wasn't going to quit myself, I figured, maybe they would and I could document their experience. Since I am on a medication at the moment that makes it inadvisable or even dangerous to drive, my mother drove, only too happy to sit in a room and listen and nod approvingly while I was catechized on the grim facts of addiction.

To be honest, it wasn't so bad. There were twenty of us lined up around the table; I was surprised to find that my time smoking, thirty-two years, didn't even come up to the median time of thirty-seven years, although it is true that most of them had a few years on me. A couple of them really didn't need to be there; they were down to two or three cigarettes a day. Hell, I fart more smoke than they breathe. Obviously our seminar leader had delivered the same talk a hundred times; the explanations came with a practiced air, the humor had a canned quality that made you realize you were hearing something repeated. Not completely a bad thing: when one woman said her car didn't even have ashtrays, our leader shot back *So you're a litterbug?* The clichés had the virtue of being for the most part true. It's true that the one about F.E.A.R. being False Evidence Appearing Real has always gotten under my skin — what about the fear of death? — but that's just me being a little close-minded. Others were *Failing to plan is planning to fail* and, in regards to smoking while angry, that *Smoking at someone is like drinking poison and expecting them to die.* And she introduced us to the concept of *euphoric recall*: that memory or association of pleasure that a smoker gets just from thinking of smoking, just like what a cokehead gets from the thought of doing a line or a compulsive eater gets from the thought of a cheeseburger. *Euphoric recall*: a useful concept.

She didn't lay down any bullshit. She didn't try to sell us on herbal remedies or hypnosis or reflexology or acupuncture. Rather, she came right out and told us these methods probably wouldn't work. She was down to earth, sensible. *Evidence-based solutions* were her emphasis. Nicotine lozenges, nicotine gum, the patch. Changing your habits. Planning ahead. Understanding the cycle of alternately drenching and starving the receptors in your brain that respond to nicotine, that flood the pleasure centers of the brain with dopamine. She made sense.

SMOKING

As a little treat at the end, she had each of us take a deep breath, hold it for fifteen seconds, then blow through a tube into a little machine that measured the carbon monoxide — one of smoke's most dangerous poisons — in our blood. Score! I got thirty-seven parts per million, easily the highest in the room.

23.

As *The Cigarette Century* has it:

The fall of the cigarette that marks the second half of the twentieth century may only be considered provisional at best. More than one in five American adults still smoke regularly, and today tobacco still kills more than 435,000 U.S. citizens each year (more than HIV, alcohol, illicit drugs, suicide, and homicide combined). Former Surgeon General C. Everett Koop, eager to translate these numbers for greater public impact, repeatedly explained that tobacco deaths equaled three 747s crashing daily for a year, with no survivors. But smokers don't die such sudden and traumatic deaths — they die, typically in hospitals, slowly, one at a time; often after extended illness and suffering; and now often ashamed, convinced they have sown their own fate. . . .

The number of deaths in the United States, however, are dwarfed by those now occurring around the world. And while many American smokers have tried to quit with some success, smoking has been on a steep increase, especially in poorer nations. As the tobacco companies lost ground in the developed world they aggressively sought new smokers in developing nations.

The global tobacco industry is not hurting. The big multinationals are not hurting. If anything, these are boom times for Big Tobacco. And to understand how very good they are, we have to look outside the United States for a moment at the rest of the world — the one hundred twenty plus countries that grow tobacco, and all the other countries which consume it.

*

According to *The Tobacco Atlas* (available as a book and in an online version at tobaccoatlas.org), "World tobacco production peaked in 1997 at over 9 million tonnes," although the amount has declined some since then, to 7.1 million tonnes in 2010. (Sometimes the world overproduces; the number of smokers, globally, is not going down.) A tonne is a metric measurement, equivalent to 1,000 kilograms or 2,205 pounds. That means that the world produced roughly 15,655,500,000 pounds of tobacco in 2010. If there are 7 billion people on the planet, that's roughly two and a quarter pounds of tobacco per person. Even more relevant, it's a shade over

13 pounds of tobacco *per smoker*. Tobacco is dried in the curing process, so it doesn't have a lot moisture in it, which means that it's pretty light; a pound of tobacco goes a long way. So thirteen pounds of tobacco, a little more than a pound per month? That's more than five hundred cigarettes a month, which is a lot of tobacco to burn and suck into your lungs.

Again according to *The Tobacco Atlas*, there are more than 500 cigarette factories around the world. If you think that smoking is in any way declining, bear in mind that those factories, whose total production is nearly 6 trillion cigarettes per year, represents an increase in total cigarette production of about 13% over a decade ago.

Since tobacco is grown almost everywhere, including most impoverished countries, it takes land that might otherwise go to food production. It's quite simple: tobacco brings in more money than food does. "In 2009," *says The Tobacco Atlas*, "six of the top ten tobacco-producing countries had undernourishment rates between 5% and 27%. In 2008 in Malawi, a top tobacco-producing country with 27% undernourishment, each hectare of land devoted to tobacco produced 1 tonne of tobacco leaf; a hectare of land growing potatoes produced 14.6 tonnes in the same year."

But that isn't the only problem with tobacco production. Tobacco farming more or less destroys the environment, whether it's from deforestation to get wood for the curing process or it's from the process of farming itself. Tobacco sucks nutrients out of the soil, which in turn leads to a need for fertilizer, some of which then runs off and pollutes the environment. Tobacco is notoriously prone to pests, which means pesticides are also used heavily, leading to yet more contaminants. Pesticides can cause neurological damage, and tobacco itself can cause nicotine poisoning when it's handled without proper protection, a condition called "green tobacco sickness." Is it worth it? Even in the United States, after layouts for equipment and supplies, farmers collect less than 1% of what consumers actually spend on tobacco.

*

Just how big an impact is tobacco having in the world right now, in the early years of the twenty-first century? Well, a CBSNews.com report of March 21, 2012 entitled "Tobacco Use Claimed 6 Million Lives in 2011, Report Shows" reported on the new version of the American Cancer Society's and World Lung Foundation's book *The Tobacco Atlas*. According to the World Lung Foundation's announcement, "In 2010, the combined profits of the six leading tobacco companies was U.S. $35.1 billion, equal to the combined profits of Coca-Cola, Microsoft, and McDonald's in the same year. If Big Tobacco were a country, it would have a gross domestic product (GDP) of countries like Poland, Saudi Arabia, Sweden and Venezuela." The report goes on to note, "When considering 2010 deaths with tobacco industry revenue, *the tobacco industry realizes almost $6,000 in profit for each death caused by tobacco.*"

$35.1 billion — that's the profits. The *profits*, not the total revenue. How much do people actually spend on tobacco? According to a World Lung Foundation report of the same date, the total amount people spend on tobacco is much, much higher. An order of magnitude higher. As the report notes, "According to *The Tobacco Atlas*, estimates of revenues from the global tobacco industry likely approach a half trillion U.S. dollars annually."

The gross domestic product of the United States, the world's biggest economy, is estimated as of 2013 to total about $13 trillion. That's the value of the whole country's products and services in a year. If the total revenues of the tobacco industry are a half trillion dollars, that means the world is spending (again, roughly) the equivalent of about 4% of U.S. GDP on tobacco.

One dollar in twenty-five of the total U.S. economy is going to tobacco, which pretty much means to smoking. And a dollar in most places is a lot of money. There are places where people make $300 dollars a year.

But the costs don't stop there, of course. And by costs we are talking about more than just money. The World Lung Foundation report goes on to note:

> Tobacco use is the number one killer in China, causing 1.2 million deaths annually; this is expected to rise to 3.5 million deaths annually by the year 2030. Tobacco is also responsible for the greatest proportion of male deaths in Turkey (38%) and Kazakhstan (35%), and the greatest proportion of female deaths in the Maldives (25%) and the United States (23%).

That's 1.2 million deaths *every single year* in China. It's like they're fighting a major war without ever declaring it. To give some perspective on 1.2 million deaths, it is roughly the same size as an American city like Dallas, Texas. It is one and a half times the size of Columbus, Ohio and twice the size of Washington, D.C. or Portland, Oregon or Oklahoma City or Milwaukee or Las Vegas. We're talking about the urban populations here, the concentrated populations of some of the biggest cities in the States. Killed by tobacco — every year. And in less than twenty years, in China that's going to triple. China, all by itself, is enduring a small holocaust. And that's just China. Around the world, about six million people — more than twice the population of Chicago — die from tobacco use every year, from smoking. In the United States alone, it's 435,000 people. That's Atlanta; that's Raleigh; that's Omaha. As summed up by the Center for Disease Control and Prevention's website, "Cigarette smoking results in 5.1 million years of potential life lost in the United States annually."

"It is now projected that in the course of the twenty-first century, one billion people across the globe will die of tobacco-related diseases," says *The Cigarette Century*. "This figure represents a ten-fold increase over the deaths associated with the cigarette in the last century."

When are people going to notice what's happening? Probably not for a while.

> "The tobacco industry thrives on ignorance of the true harms of tobacco use and using misinformation to subvert health policies that could save millions," said Peter Baldini, chief executive officer, World Lung Foundation.

The cigarette companies are never going to own up to the situation — that's clear. It took how long for them to admit something as simple, as patently obvious, as scientifically proven as the fact that nicotine is addictive? The fact that cigarettes might be harmful? Public health officials and concerned citizens hammered away at these issues for decades, while Big Tobacco issued nothing but straight-faced denials. I am not in a position to criticize — I *am* a smoker, after all — but we would be fools to expect them to suddenly make any sort of about-face admission regarding the scale of the current holocaust. We — ourselves, our friends and our families, the members of a responsible media — we are going to have to spread the word ourselves, over and over and over again, until the message finally gets through.

24.

A few years back I had to be in the hospital for about a week and a half. During this time there was no smoking. There was no way for me even to get outside if I wanted to smoke, let alone anything as convenient as a smoking room somewhere. It was a completely smoke-free environment. To keep me from going into convulsions and making my condition even worse, they gave me a nicotine patch. And the truth is, it was surprisingly effective. Every morning they would come into my room and peel off the old depleted patch and slap on a new nicotine-rich patch. Every day I had a nice continuous stream of nicotine flowing into my system. Sure, I missed lighting up a cigarette, sucking the smoke into my lungs, all the little habits that go with smoking. But it got me through. And to be honest, I was fine with it. In fact, after a few days I didn't even think about smoking. I felt great. Every morning I had been reminding the nurse first thing to get me my patch, but after a week I didn't even care. I stopped asking for it and they forgot or simply neglected to give it to me. And I quit just like that.

I made sure my mother, though, who was coming to pick me up when I got out, didn't forget to bring me a pack of cigarettes. It wasn't that I really wanted to smoke; it was just that I wanted to be sure, the comfort of knowing I had them. And to be honest, the idea of a cigarette didn't seem half so bad. Wouldn't it be nice just to have just *one*? What the hell, why not? One little smoke couldn't hurt me.

The day came and they let me out of the hospital. We were headed for the door and I asked her if she'd remembered to bring my butts. *Sure*, she said, reaching into her purse, *here they are*.

I whipped off the wrapper like a bulimic going into a box of chocolates. I wasn't halfway across the parking lot before I had that sucker lit up.

The Little White Slaver they used to call it. And believe me, they aren't kidding.

I've been smoking like a chimney ever since.

*

So I am an unrepentant smoker. More: I revel in it. I won't say I love it, but when I picture life without it,

SMOKING

I admit that the future seems a little impoverished, the colors a little faded. I'm not yet ready to quit. And cutting down has never worked for me. When I smoke, I'm in all the way.

As much as I know about tobacco, about what cigarettes do and how they are made, about what chemicals go into and come out of them, I will admit that I really don't care. Oh, *intellectually* I understand. But do I *really* understand? It is as though there is a giant mental blind spot screening out all thought of the future: heart disease, cancer, emphysema, a host of other ailments. It is a failure of the imagination, a failure to grasp the reality of the world: that what you do has consequences. Seven minutes for every cigarette, they say: that's what each butt takes off your life. Hell, I should be dead by now. Maybe — just maybe — my time is right around the corner, and me, poor me, I don't even realize it. *He was so young. What a shame. Oh you didn't know? Yeah, he was a smoker.* The average smoker loses fourteen years of his life, and I smoke more than the average. For me it's looking more like twenty.

Smokers play a kind of lottery, just as real and consequential as playing the one for money. More consequential really: winning a million bucks may be great but it can't give you back those lost twenty years. And your odds of winning the smokers' lottery are a lot higher — almost a certainty, in fact. Half of all smokers die of a smoking-related illness. In the race between whatever your lifestyle and your genetics have be-queathed you and smoking, smoking wins half the time. And when you're dead, you're gone. That's what it comes down to. Never mind the six months or six years of suffering first, combined with the terrible knowledge that you did all this to yourself.

Someday I'll quit but for now, well, I'm just going to coast along for a while. And guess what? A friend of mine sold me on Rolling Your Own — RYO is what the industry calls it. They have these little machines you use; it's easy. I can roll a pack in just a few minutes. It's even kind of entertaining. You just stuff the to-bacco into the machine, stick on a tube — filter al-ready attached — and crank the arm and voilá! Instant cigarette. It's saving me 250 bucks a month. Hell, even with the tax increase that's coming — it's in the pipeline now — I can afford these kinds of cigarettes no sweat. The machine — forty bucks — plus enough tobacco for two cartons of cigarettes and the tubes cost me less than I paid for *one carton* of my old brand. And the machine was two-thirds of the cost — I don't have to pay that again. This is a game-changer. My mother was so impressed with the savings that the first thing she did was tell her boyfriend about it; as soon as he came over we all went out and found him a machine. I was like a used-car salesman taking him out through the lot; my two days of experience made me an expert. *This is a really good machine,* I said. *See how it's made of metal? That's industrial-grade.* My mother got into the action and bought him his first big bag of tobacco. My mother? Spending money *on tobacco?* But no — he just didn't like this brand — not full-flavor enough, he said. So what did she do? She went out and bought him some more. A couple of smaller ones so he could try them out and find the one that he likes. Guess who got the stuff he didn't like? Score! Tastes just fine to me.

And when I said it's a game-changer, I wasn't kidding. When you live on a fairly limited budget like I do — I'm not poor but I'm sure not rich either — that quarter or third of your income going into butts just isn't funny. I don't remember the last time I could smoke a cigarette without feeling a little stress about what it was costing; how at the end of the month I had to worry about the bank, about getting from day to day. I paid for a friend's lunch the other day — it wasn't a cheap lunch either — and when was the last time I did that? I bought when the family went out for sundaes — not just my share but everyone's. And I didn't have to think about it. It's been years since I had this kind of money, all because of the way cigarettes were bleeding me dry. Now I can light up with ease, jingle the coins in my pocket and quit thinking about it.

I know that the clock is ticking: that sooner or later I'm going to have to get serious about my smoking. But just let me enjoy it a little longer. Illusive it may be but it feels — it *feels* — like I could go on like this forever.

Acknowledgments

I wrote this book simply because I was curious about smoking. I had no agenda. As a lifelong smoker, I was, if anything, pro-tobacco. Learning about smoking — and about the history of the tobacco industry in particular — has certainly been an education.

I consulted many sources in my study of this topic, many of them quite excellent. Most of them dealt with only a narrow aspect of the subject, however, which is only natural: a truly comprehensive history of smoking would take many thousands of pages. Thankfully I was able to locate three books in particular which helped to broaden my picture of and clarify my thinking about the story of tobacco and cigarettes. These are the sources I quote from most often, as they often elucidate points in ways that I saw no need to improve on. These three books are: Iain Gately's *Tobacco: A Cultural History of How an Exotic Plant Seduced Civilization*, Jordan Goodman's *Tobacco In History: The Cultures of Dependence* and Allen M. Brandt's *The Cigarette Century: The Rise, Fall, and Deadly Persistence of the Product That Defined America*. It is hard to imagine books that are better written or better researched; these are books written on a heroic scale. If you only want to read one book on smoking, however, and are less interested in tobacco's early history than in the modern era, the book to read is probably Richard Kluger's Pulitzer Prize-winning *Ashes to Ashes: America's Hundred-Year Cigarette War, the Public Health, and the Unabashed Triumph of Philip Morris*. This weighty tome, which comes in at around 750 closely printed pages in paperback, covers many of the diverse aspects of cigarettes and smoking in enough detail that it will satisfy any lingering curiosity you may have about such subjects as the development of the modern cigarette companies, cigarette advertising and marketing, the emergence of the science that shows that smoking is harmful, the development of the filter (an interesting side topic unto itself) and how cigarette companies are adapting to the modern era. My only regret is that the book was published in the late 1990s and doesn't cover recent developments. Hopefully it will be updated soon.

Several readers looked at this book while it was in progress and shared their thoughts with me on how it could be improved. These people were extremely generous with their time and I appreciate their insights. They include Mark Bonica, Heidi Ripley Fowler, Kevin Carney, Samanthe Lund Newell, Pam Wurzel Nichols, John Rossey, and Beth Sundermeyer.

ACKNOWLEDGMENTS

I also owe a particular debt of gratitude to Danny O'Malley for sharing his personal insights into the nature of lung cancer and emphysema. They helped turn what might seem abstract medical information into a human picture that I — and hopefully you — could understand and relate to.

Appendix 1: Varieties of Tobacco

I am not an expert on tobacco. There are many varieties of tobacco grown in various parts of the world. Some kinds of tobacco are named not for the strain of tobacco but for the process used in curing, manufacturing or some other part of the process. In researching this book I found it difficult to find any comprehensive or informative list of the varieties of tobacco. Most references to a specific variety of tobacco in the literature are somewhat mystifying due to this lack of information. You will most likely not find any information about what varieties of tobacco are used in a pack of cigarettes, but this does not mean that this information is not important; manufacturers blend different varieties to create the unique flavors of different brands (not that most people can tell the difference). This list, taken almost directly from the Wikipedia article 'Types of tobacco' with a few minor edits on my part and some additions derived from my reading, is the most informative that I have found.

Note that all varieties of commercial tobacco belong to the species *Nicotiana tabacum*, commonly called 'tabacum,' or *Nicotiana rustica,* commonly called 'rustica.' Both are native to the Americas, as noted in Chapter 3.

This appendix is provided purely for the convenience of the reader and is not meant to be comprehensive; for instance, there is a website called sustainable-seedco.com that currently offers 96 varieties of tobacco seeds, many of them heirloom tobaccos, beginning with *African Red* and running down through the alphabet to *Yellow Prior.* The list below consists of some of the most commonly used varieties. Check Wikipedia for updates.

Definitions of the various terms for curing, such as 'fire curing,' 'air curing,' etc., may be found in Appendix 2: Growing and Curing Tobacco.

*

Aromatic Fire-cured. Usually simply called 'fire-cured,' this tobacco is cured by smoke from open fires. In the United States, it is grown in northern middle Tennessee, central Kentucky and in Virginia. Fire-cured tobacco grown in Kentucky and Tennessee are used in some chewing tobaccos, moist snuff, some cigarettes, and as a condiment in pipe tobacco blends.

Brightleaf (or most often simply 'Bright') is commonly known as 'Virginia,' often regardless of which state in which it is planted. Prior to the American Civil War, most tobacco grown in the US was fire-cured dark-leaf. This dark-leaf tobacco was planted in fertile lowlands, used a robust variety of leaf, and was either fire cured or air cured.

Sometime after the War of 1812, demand for a milder, lighter, more aromatic tobacco arose. Ohio, Pennsylvania and Maryland all innovated with milder varieties of the tobacco plant. Farmers around the country experimented with different curing processes. But the breakthrough did not come until around 1839.

Growers had noticed that sandy, highland soil produced thinner, weaker plants. Captain Abisha Slade of Caswell County, North Carolina had considerable infertile, sandy soil, and planted the new 'gold-leaf' varieties on it. Slade owned a slave, Stephen, who around 1839 accidentally produced the first true Bright tobacco. He used charcoal to restart a fire used to cure the crop. The surge of heat turned the leaves yellow. Using that discovery, Slade developed a system for producing Bright tobacco, cultivated on poorer soils and using charcoal for heat-curing.

Slade made many public appearances to share the Bright-leaf process with other farmers. His success helped him build a brick house in Yanceyville, North Carolina, and at one time he had many servants.

News spread through the area pretty quickly. The infertile sandy soil of the Appalachian piedmont was suddenly profitable, and people rapidly developed flue-curing techniques, a more efficient way of smoke-free curing. Farmers discovered that Bright leaf tobacco needs thin, starved soil, and those who could not grow other crops found that they could grow tobacco. Formerly unproductive farms reached 20–35 times their previous worth. By 1855, six Piedmont counties adjoining Virginia ruled the tobacco market.

By the outbreak of the Civil War, the town of Danville, Virginia had developed a Bright-leaf market for the surrounding area in Caswell Country, North Carolina and Pittsylvania County, Virginia.

Danville was also the main railway head for Confederate soldiers going to the front. These brought Bright tobacco with them from Danville to the lines, traded it with each other and Union soldiers, and developed quite a taste for it. At the end of the war, the soldiers went home and a national market had developed for the local crop. Caswell and Pittsylvania counties were the only two counties in the South that increased in total wealth after the war.

Most Canadian cigarettes are made from 100% pure Virginia tobacco.

Burley is a light air-cured tobacco used primarily for cigarette production. In the United States, it is produced in an eight-state belt with approximately 70% produced in Kentucky. Tennessee produces approximately 20%, with smaller amounts produced in Indiana, North Carolina, Missouri, Ohio, Virginia and West Virginia. Burley tobacco is produced in many other countries, with major production in Brazil, Malawi and Argentina. In the U.S., Burley tobacco plants are started from palletized seeds placed in polystyrene trays floated on a bed of fertilized water in March or April. In 1880 Kentucky produced 36% of the total national tobacco production, and was first in the country, with nearly twice as much tobacco produced as by Virginia, then the second-place state.

The origin of White Burley is credited to a Mr. Webb in 1864, who grew it near Higginsport in Brown County, Ohio from Red Burley seed he had purchased from Bracken County, Kentucky. After he planted the seed he found that a few of the seedlings had a whitish, sickly look. He transplanted them to the fields anyway, where they grew into mature plants but retained their light color; it yielded a different type of light leaf shaded from white to yellow and it cured differently. The cured leaves had an exceedingly fine texture and were exhibited as a curiosity at the market in Cincinnati. The following year he planted ten acres from seeds from those plants, which brought a premium at auction. The air-cured leaf was found to be mild tasting and more absorbent than any other variety. By 1866, he harvested 20,000 pounds of this Burley tobacco and sold it in 1867 at the St. Louis Fair for $58 per hundred pounds. By 1883, the principal market for this tobacco was Cincinnati, but it was grown throughout central Kentucky and Middle Tennessee. White Burley, as it was later called, became the main component in chewing tobacco, American blend pipe tobacco, and American-style cigarettes. The 'white' part of the name is seldom used today, since Red Burley, a dark air-cured variety of the mid-19th century, no longer exists.

Cavendish is more a process of curing and a method of cutting tobacco than a type of it. The processing and the cut are used to bring out the natural sweet taste in the tobacco. Cavendish can be produced out of any tobacco type but is usually one of, or a blend of, Kentucky, Virginia, and Burley and is most commonly used for pipe tobacco and cigars.

The process begins by pressing the tobacco leaves into a cake about an inch thick. Heat from fire or steam is applied, and the tobacco is allowed to ferment. This is said to result in a sweet and mild tobacco. Finally the cake is sliced. These slices must be broken apart, as by rubbing in a circular motion between one's palms, before the tobacco can be evenly packed into a pipe. Flavoring is often added before the leaves are pressed. English Cavendish uses a dark flue- or fire-cured Virginia (DEC), which is steamed and then stored under pressure to permit it to cure and ferment for several days or weeks.

Corojo is a type of tobacco primarily used in the making of cigars, originally grown in the Vuelta Abajo region of Cuba.

Corojo was originally developed and grown by Diego Rodriguez at his farm or vega, Santa Ines del Corojo and takes its name from the farm. It was used as a wrapper extensively for many years on Cuban cigars, but its susceptibility to various diseases, blue mold in particular, caused the Cuban genetic engineers to develop various hybrid forms that would not only be disease-resistant, but would also display excellent wrapper qualities.

Criollo is a type of tobacco primarily used in the making of cigars. It was, by most accounts, one of the original Cuban tobaccos that emerged around the time of Columbus.

The term means *native seed*, and thus a tobacco variety using the term, such as *Dominican Criollo*, may or may not have anything to do with the original Cuban seed nor the recent hybrid, *Criollo '98*.

Dokham is a tobacco of Iranian origin mixed with leaves, bark, and herbs for smoking in a midwakh.

Latakia is a fire-cured tobacco and is produced from Oriental varieties of *Nicotiana tabacum*. The leaves are cured and smoked over smoldering fires of local hardwoods and aromatic shrubs in Cyprus and Syria.

Oriental is a sun-cured, highly aromatic, small-leafed variety (*Nicotiana tabacum*) that is grown in Turkey, Greece, Bulgaria, and Macedonia. Oriental tobacco is frequently referred to as 'Turkish tobacco,' as these regions were all historically part of the Ottoman Empire. Many of the early brands of cigarettes were made mostly or entirely of Oriental tobacco; today, its main use is in blends of pipe and especially cigarette tobacco (a typical American cigarette is a blend of Bright Virginia, Burley and Oriental).

Perique. Perhaps the most strongly flavored of all tobaccos is the Perique, from Saint James Parish, Louisiana. When the Acadians made their way into this region in 1755, the Choctaw and Chickasaw tribes were cultivating a variety of tobacco with a distinctive flavor. A farmer called Pierre Chenet is credited with first turning this local tobacco into the Perique in 1824 through the technique of pressure-fermentation.

Considered the truffle of pipe tobaccos, it is used as a component in many blended pipe tobaccos but is too strong to be smoked pure. At one time, the freshly moist Perique was also chewed, but none is now sold for this purpose. It is typically blended with pure Virginia to lend spice, strength and coolness to the blend.

Shade tobacco. It is not well known that the northern US states of Connecticut and Massachusetts are also two of the most important tobacco-growing regions in the country. Long before Europeans arrived in the area, Native Americans cultivated tobacco along the banks of the Connecticut River. Today, the Connecticut River valley north of Hartford, Connecticut is known as 'Tobacco Valley,' and the fields and drying sheds are visible to travelers on the road to and from Bradley International Airport, the major Connecticut airport.

Connecticut shade tobacco is grown under tents to protect plant leaves from direct sunlight. This imitates the conditions of tobacco plants growing in the shade of trees in tropical areas. The results are leaves of lighter color and of a more delicate structure. They are used as outer wrappers for some of the world's finest cigars. It is not entirely clear who introduced this method of growing tobacco, but it is likely that the New York firm of Schroeder & Bon or its founder Frederick A. Schroeder were instrumental in developing this agricultural innovation.

Early Connecticut colonists acquired from the Native Americans the habit of smoking tobacco in pipes and began cultivating the plant commercially even though the Puritans referred to it as the 'evil weed.' The plant was outlawed in Connecticut in 1650, but in the 19th century, as cigar smoking began to be popular, tobacco farming became a major industry, employing farmers, laborers, local youths, southern African Americans, and migrant workers.

Working conditions varied from back-breaking work for young local children, ages 13 and up, to back-breaking exploitation of migrants. Each tobacco plant yields only 18 leaves useful as cigar wrappers, and each leaf requires a great deal of individual manual attention during harvesting. Although the temperature in the curing sheds sometimes exceeds 38° C (100° F), no work is done inside the sheds while the tobacco is being fired.

In 1921, Connecticut tobacco production peaked at 31,000 acres under cultivation. The rise of cigarette smoking and the decline of cigar smoking have caused a corresponding decline in the demand for shade tobacco, reaching a minimum in 1992 of 2,000 acres under cultivation. Since then, however, cigar smoking has become more popular again, and in 1997 tobacco farming had risen to 4,000 acres. However, only 1,050 acres of shade tobacco were harvested in the Connecticut Valley in 2006. Connecticut seed is being grown in Ecuador, where labor is very cheap. Historically, the industry has weathered some major catastrophes, including a devastating hailstorm in 1929 and an epidemic of brown spot fungus in 2000, but is now in danger of disappearing altogether given the value of the land to real-estate speculators. The older and much less labor-intensive Broad leaf plant, which produces an excellent Mauro wrapper as well as binder and filler for cigars, is increasing in area in the Connecticut Valley.

Type 22 tobacco is a classification of United States tobacco product as defined by the U.S. Department of Agriculture, effective date November 7, 1986. The definition states that type 22 tobacco is a type of dark fire-cured tobacco, known as Eastern District fire-cured, produced principally in a section east of the Tennessee River in southern Kentucky and northern Tennessee. Most type 22 tobacco in northern Tennessee is grown in Robertson and Montgomery County. Its principal use is in the manufacture of chewing tobacco.

Wild tobacco is native to the southwestern United States, Mexico, and parts of South America. It belongs to the

Nicotiana rustica genus. In Australia, *Nicotiana benthamiana* and *Nicotiana gossei* are two of several indigenous tobaccos still used by Aboriginal people in some areas. *Nicotiana rustica* is the most potent strain of tobacco known. As a smoking tobacco, it is mostly used in Asia. It is commonly used for tobacco dust or pesticides.

Y-1 is a strain of tobacco that was crossbred by tobacco giant Brown & Williamson to obtain an unusually high nicotine content. It became controversial in the 1990s when the United States Food and Drug Administration (FDA) used it as evidence that tobacco companies were intentionally manipulating the nicotine content of cigarettes.

Y-1 was developed by tobacco plant researcher James Chaplin, working under Dr. Jeffrey Wigand, who would later blow the whistle on Brown & Williamson in a famous *60 Minutes* interview and who later claimed he had received death threats for what he had done (for more information, see the article on Wikipedia). Chaplin and Wigand worked for Brown & Williamson (then a subsidiary of British American Tobacco) in the late 1970s. Chaplin, a director of the USDA Research Laboratory at Oxford, North Carolina, had described the need for a higher nicotine tobacco plant in the trade publication *World Tobacco* in 1977 and had bred a number of high-nicotine strains based on a hybrid of

Nicotiana tabacum and *Nicotiana rustica*, but the plants were weak and would blow over in a strong wind. Only two grew to maturity; Y-2, which 'turned black in the drying barn and smelled like old socks,' and Y-1, which was a success.

B&W brought the plants to California company DNA Plant Technology for additional modification, including making the plants male-sterile, a procedure that prevents competitors from reproducing the strain from seeds. DNA Plant Technology then smuggled the seeds to a B&W subsidiary in Brazil.

Y-1 has a higher nicotine content than conventional flue-cured tobacco (6.5% versus 3.2–3.5%), but a comparable amount of tar, and it does not affect taste or aroma. British American Tobacco (BAT) began to discuss the trialing of Y1 tobacco in 1991, despite it not being approved for use in the United States. B&W promised in 1994 to stop using Y-1, but at that time they had 7 million pounds of inventory and continued to blend Y-1 into their products until 1999.

Appendix 2: Growing and Curing Tobacco

Growing Tobacco

As noted in Chapter 7, growing tobacco is a labor-intensive business and, in traditional agriculture, careful hands-on work is required at every stage of the process. The work goes on through much of the year and requires much manual labor. In Chapter 7 I quoted Jordan Goodman's *Tobacco In History: The Cultures of Dependence* on what this process was like until recent times in America (and remains like in much of the world), until the introduction of certain labor-saving machines and chemicals; for the reader's convenience, I repeat the quotation here.

> Tobacco cultivation in the seventeenth century absorbed about half of the year's working time. The slackest time of the year was between January and early April during which time the seedbeds were being made and tended. In these months, typically the only time in the year when workers could afford some leisure time, only about 10 per cent of available working time was used on the fledgling plants.

In April, however, labour demands rose enormously. Transplanting absorbed virtually the entire working schedule in both April and May. Some respite came in June when weeds began to appear in the fields, but in July and August topping, suckering and weeding left workers with no time for leisure. September, October and November were somewhat less demanding, but even then cutting, stripping, stemming and prizing absorbed, on average, 50 per cent of the entire working schedule.

Tobacco cultivation was often merciless with labour. The planter, as we have seen, did not escape lightly. Even if he did not work in the fields — a rare event in the Chesapeake with the possible exception of the very big landowners — his consciousness, if not his hands, was always involved in critical decisions. . . . Different kinds of skills were displayed throughout the year within an unchanging regime of extreme careful handling. The most skilled work occurred in cutting and in prizing. The cutter did not just perform an intensive task — each plant had to be cut separately and handed carefully to someone who would gather several plants at a time — but he had to make decisions in the field as to which plants to cut and precisely where to make the incision. Prizing was an activity that required considerable judgement and acquaintance with the materials. The object of prizing was literally to stuff a wooden barrel with as many layers of tobacco leaf as possible without rupturing the container. These hogsheads of tobacco were exceedingly heavy. . . . What came out of the hogsheads on the other side of the Atlantic [i.e., the quality of the tobacco] was the result not only of the curing stage but more importantly of prizing. Planters were under a strong incentive to pack the hogsheads to breaking point since freight rates were reckoned on the number not the weight of hogsheads.

In much of the world, where traditional methods are still used, the process remains much the same. The main changes in modern tobacco production have mostly come in the form of machines and chemicals, detailed with the growing terms below.

Growing Terms

Seedbeds. Tobacco was traditionally planted in seedbeds or in containers with some sort of protection from insects and the elements, such as in a greenhouse or under a frame covered with a fabric like cotton or linen. Tobacco seeds are almost microscopic; it takes about 80,000 to make one ounce of seeds. Because they are so small, the seeds are mixed with soil, which is then spread over the top of the beds; the goal is to achieve an even distribution.

Transplanting. Just what it sounds like — the plants are taken from the seedbeds (or containers) out to the fields. They are spaced about two to three feet apart in mounded rows to give them room to grow.

Weeding. Like other crops, tobacco fields need to be weeded. In modern times, chemicals have made this a much easier process.

Fertilizing. Also like other crops, tobacco fields need to be fertilized, and since tobacco tends to deplete soil rapidly this especially important. Note: tobacco is seldom given nitrogen, as starving the plant of this nutrient helps to produce the lighter-flavored, yellow tobacco most people prefer.

Topping is the process of removing the flowers once they appear. This has the effect of concentrating the plant's energy into the growth of the rest of the plant.

Suckering is the process of removing secondary growths or shoots, known as suckers, from the plant. Like topping, this has the effect of concentrating the plant's energy into the growth of the rest of the plant. In modern times, chemicals have been produced which kill off suckers and save much time in what was previously a labor-intensive process.

Cutting. Before the twentieth century, tobacco was usually harvested by cutting down the whole plant. This had the result of harvesting some leaves which were not a their peak of development. In modern times this has been replaced by the removal of the leaves one at a time as each ripens.

Stripping. Stripping is the removing of the leaves from the stalk.

Prizing. In the old days, this was the process of stuffing a hogshead as full of layers of tobacco as possible. The idea was to do it without ruining the tobacco in the process, which required some skill. Hogsheads were used to ship tobacco to England and later other destinations. This method has since been replaced by more modern methods of shipping.

*

Curing Tobacco

The information which follows is taken more or less directly from the Wikipedia article 'Curing of tobacco,' with some minor edits and additions on my part. Again, this information is not meant to be comprehensive; it is supplied simply for the convenience of the reader.

Processes

After tobacco has been harvested, it is necessary to cure it — essentially, drying the leaf to a desired degree of moisture — before consumption. Curing and subsequent aging allow for the slow oxidation and degradation of carotenoids in the tobacco leaf. This produces various compounds in the tobacco leaves that give cured tobacco its sweet hay, tea, rose oil, or fruity aromatic flavor that contributes to the smoothness of the consumed product. Non-aged or low-quality tobacco is often artificially flavored with these otherwise naturally occurring compounds. Tobacco flavoring is a significant source of revenue for the international multi-million dollar flavor and fragrance industry.

After tobacco is cured, it is moved from the curing barn into a storage area for processing. If whole plants were cut, the leaves are removed from the tobacco stalks in a process called *stripping*. For both cut and pulled tobacco, the leaves are then sorted into different grades. In colonial times, the tobacco was then *prized* into hogsheads for transportation. In Bright-tobacco regions, prizing was replaced by stacking wrapped *hands* (a bundle of leaves) into loose piles to be sold at auction. Today, most cured tobacco is baled before sales are made under pre-sold contracts.

Methods

Cut plants or pulled leaves are usually transferred immediately to tobacco barns (kiln houses), where they will be cured. Curing methods vary with the type of tobacco grown, and tobacco barn design varies accordingly. In recent times traditional curing barns in the U.S. have been falling into disuse, as the trend toward using prefabricated metal curing boxes continues. Temporary curing boxes are often found on location on tobacco farms.

Air-cured tobacco is hung in well-ventilated barns and allowed to dry over a period of four to eight weeks. Air-cured tobacco is low in sugar, which gives the tobacco smoke a light, sweet flavor, and a high nicotine content. Cigar and Burley tobaccos are air cured.

Fire-cured tobacco is hung in large barns where fires of hardwoods are kept on continuous or intermittent low smoulder and takes between three days and ten weeks, depending on the process and the tobacco. Fire curing produces a tobacco low in sugar and high in nicotine.

Pipe tobacco, chewing tobacco and snuff are fire cured.

Flue-cured tobacco was originally strung onto tobacco sticks, which were hung from tier-poles in curing barns (Australia: kilns, also traditionally called 'oasts'). These barns have flues which run from externally fed fireboxes, heat-curing the tobacco without exposing it to smoke, slowly raising the temperature over the course of the curing. The process will generally take about a week. This method produces cigarette tobacco that is high in sugar and has medium to high levels of nicotine.

Sun-cured tobacco dries uncovered in the sun. This method is used in Turkey, Greece, Bulgaria, Macedonia, Romania and the Mediterranean countries to produce Oriental tobacco. Sun-cured tobacco is low in sugar and nicotine and is used in cigarettes. In India sun curing is used to produce so-called 'white' snuffs, which are fine, dry and unusually potent.

ABOUT THE AUTHOR

Eric Coates grew up in New Hampshire. He attended Bard College and lived in numerous cities, including New York, San Francisco and Portland, Oregon. *Smoking* is his third book. His other books include *Hearing Voices: A Memoir of Madness; Cracking Up: A Memoir of Love, Drinking, Drugs, Poverty, Paranoia and Other Afflictions of a Life on the Road to Madness*; and *Memos: Advice to a Young Executive on the Art of Lying, Twisting the Facts, and Using the Media for Your Own Selfish Purposes.*

www.ingramcontent.com/pod-product-compliance
Lightning Source LLC
Chambersburg PA
CBHW070418290526
45791CB00005B/1744